I Know Why Mama Cried

a memoir

Goya Spry AND Marshall Feaster

WISE INK

Scripture Resources: Biblehub.com, Biblegateway.com, and kingjamesbibleonline.org

ISBN: 978-1-63489-299-5
Library of Congress Catalog Number 2019916506

Printed in the United States of America
First Printing: 2019

23   22   21   20   19   5   4   3   2   1

Cover and interior design by Kim Morehead

Wise Ink Creative Publishing
807 Broadway St. NE, Suite 46
Minneapolis, MN 55413
www.wiseink.com

Dedication

In Loving Memory of Our Dear Mother

Thank you for your unconditional love.
We are so honored to be your daughters.

With love to each of our wonderful children, other family members, and friends for their inspiration and support.

Contents

Acknowledgments

GOYA

To my daughter and son, who have been sources of support and strength. I am grateful for your unwavering love and encouragement to pursue my endeavors, even when I told you a few years ago that I had begun writing notes for this important book. Your response will never be forgotten. I certainly appreciate you, Marshall, for your coauthorship of this book and for the books we will write together in the future. Life would have been harder to live without your *unconditional* love and support. I am grateful for "family and friends," and God is unquestionably my *ultimate source* of **everything good and perfect.**

MARSHALL

Thank you, God, for giving us the vision and means to write this first book in our series. And Goya, thank you for being my constant source of love, support, and encouragement.

Special thanks to my son and daughters: ILYATT NMW. (I always close with this acronym: *I Love You All the Time No Matter What,* period.)

To Mama: Thank you for always believing that I could do and be anything, even when I didn't believe in myself. I wonder if you knew how much I depended on your strength, your resolve, your absolute steadfast integrity, and your belief in God. God is my protector.

Finally, I would like to acknowledge with gratitude the support and love of my family, especially Roger, who always encouraged me to write even though he had no idea about the pain and suffering in remembering my childhood. They all kept me going, and this book would not have been possible without them.

Goya and Marshall

It's been a pleasure to work with Wise Ink Creative Publishing as their experts have given us guidance and insight. We want to thank everyone who worked closely with us to make sure that our combined story was told—in the way we envisioned—to bring the reader along on our family journey.

About the Authors

This book is based on the sisters' best recollection of relationships and events at the time.

Goya Spry

Goya is a first-time published author. She suppressed writing a book for many years but has been a freelance writer for a few resources throughout her adulthood. Goya is a podcaster and also a blogger with a diverse, international audience. She's a Christian, a college graduate, a mother of two, and a grandmother. She is currently working on her second book.

Marshall Feaster

Marshall is the top of the bottom half of Mama's twelve children. Retired, she spends most of her time caring for her three granddaughters. She enjoys traveling all over the world with her children, grandchildren, and Goya.

———————————

Goya and Marshall are currently working on the second book in their series, *I Know Why Mama Cried: A Collaboration Between Goya Spry and Marshall Feaster.*

Authors' Note

When we were children, we saw Mama cry often. She thought that she was crying privately, but that was not the case. Most children are observant, and when we were an "ear-shot" away from someone in emotional pain, we could usually sense it. Children see and hear things but may not say anything because they cannot comprehend what they are experiencing—and they often store it for later processing. We often heard her crying in her bedroom, or would see her wiping her eyes at any given moment—on any given day. On occasion, one of us would open her bathroom or bedroom door and might see her looking out the window, wiping her tears. When we'd ask her what was wrong, her usual answer was, "I'm okay," or, "Nothing." Many times, that made us cry too, but she didn't know it.

We cried privately for her, wondering where her tears were coming from, but deep in our hearts, it didn't matter where they came from—because Mama's pain became ours. We wanted to help but didn't know how.

The purpose of this memoir is first to honor our mother's legacy to excel—despite adversity, while maintaining strength and faith that better days are coming. Second, to encourage others who have endured or currently endure any form of abuse; and third, to prayerfully inspire them to "safely" get out of the situation, thus saving themselves and their children. We want you to trust God and to stand trustingly on His promise that He will guide you if you faithfully trust Him. There is always hope for a better life whenever God is kept at the forefront of your life.

The people in this story reflect this truth. The intent is not to mock any person's life nor hurt them in any way. Now, as grown women, having experienced our own struggles, *we know why Mama cried*. Her tears weren't always from sadness. Joy can be an equal partner to fallen tears; joy lives in the heart too, but for many, it is experienced less often than sadness, until God is "introduced" and permanently befriended.

Marshall

BORN 1955

My earliest memory is as a five-year-old in 1960. Mama and my big sister Emma were preparing me for first grade the following year. Back then, we didn't have kindergarten in the South, so they taught me to read and do arithmetic (as it was called back then, not math). Every time I got a word wrong or gave the wrong answer for a problem, Mama or my big sister would twist my ears or drive a knuckle against my temple. The lesson: Don't mess up; don't get anything wrong. From the very beginning, I learned to be afraid; I spoke softly, almost inaudibly, in case I said the wrong thing. I preferred the safety of having a chance to change my response than subjecting myself to being chastised, or worse.

I didn't know it then, but I was to become the anchor of the top half of the bottom six of Mama's twelve children. The bottom six were a lot closer, fought harder, and grew to expect more from ourselves, from others, and from the world around us. And I was the elder of this group.

If you're wondering why my story begins at age five but Goya's story begins at her birth, it is because I cannot remember any events from before I was five, but I can remember Goya from her birth and beyond. Someone else will have to tell my story from my birth to five years old.

Sometime before I started first grade, Mama ran away to Boston almost 200 miles north to find work. She wanted to get away from Daddy's weekend beatings and drunken tirades to find work and provide clothing, shoes, and other necessities for us. As a timid six-year-old, I was even more scared when she left. I had no one to get me ready for school or help me with my schoolwork—and, most importantly for me, I had no one to comb my long, red, coarse, unruly hair. I remember the first big box of clothes, shoes, and supplies she sent us. Mama even sent me a brown leather book satchel (as Mama called it) to start school. I didn't have it very long because brother Elijah was leaving the area and moving to the big city, and he asked me if he could have it.

Elijah ran his fingers across the flap of the briefcase, which even came with a large, brass-plated key, and I saw in him a longing. He was only fifteen, short like Daddy, and unsure of himself, not nearly a man yet but knowing that he had to leave. He asked, "Gusta, can I have it?" It looked like a briefcase to him. I wanted to tell him no, but knew I couldn't do it. I wanted him to have any help he needed in the Big City. Elijah said he needed it to go to school and look for work. I think he wanted to look the part of a young man who wanted to be successful.

Under those circumstances and in my young mind, I thought he needed it more than I. I gave it to him, of course, because even at age six, I thought this briefcase could help him. "Take it, Elijah," I said. The relief in his eyes was all I needed to part ways with Mama's precious gift. I would worry every day about what Mama would say when she came back home and found out that I had given it away. Even though Elijah was a scant nine years older, as I watched him walk up the hill toward the big city carrying my brown leather satchel, he looked like a lawyer from behind. I hoped that Mama would understand why I had given it to Elijah. Years later, Mama would recall that that act served as a beacon of the kind of daughter, sister, and mother I would become. As I reminisce, seeing Elijah walk away never to return and live with us again, fresh tears roll down my cheeks every single time.

Mama sent Charlotte, Olivia, and me underwear, socks, dresses, leather shoes, and coats, and Matthew and David got pants, shirts, underwear, socks, coats, and shoes too. We were happy. We thought we were rich with so many new things to wear. We had never gotten anything new before, and until then we'd only had one of everything. In fact, we had to wash our single outfit every day in the same babbling brook where we got our drinking water. The water was always cold and the wooded area was cool even in summer. There were frogs and tadpoles in abundance. I still remember the one dress I owned. It was short-sleeved with a lavender plaid skirt and a matching lavender bodice that had a purple bow and a rhinestone in the center. My sisters and brothers and I would sit on the rocks with the sun peeking through over the tree tops, worrying about how we would get through to the next day.

It's a miracle that we were never sick or that we didn't freeze to death one of those cold winters. I don't even remember having a cold, a fever, a headache, or an upset stomach. I guess God thought we had enough to deal with and He was not going to put anything more on us. He knew we had all we could bear. The truth is God never promised not to put more on us than we can handle. He promises to guide us through whatever we face.

Tears on the Muddy Dirt Hill

The ear-twisting that Mama and Emma did while teaching me to read and learn arithmetic was nothing compared to what I got from Daddy one Friday evening when I was six. At the time, Daddy was the best brick mason around Monday morning through Friday at knock-off time, but he was a drunk and abusive toward Mama and us Friday through Sunday. Daddy was known by family and friends — he may have been short in stature, but he packed a mean punch when he was abusive. He was only about 5' 5", but his actions were bigger than life in terms of the way they negatively impacted his family's lives. He had the ability to strike fear in all of us with just a look. We all knew what could follow that look. I remember many times watching Daddy beat Mama, helpless to do anything about it. We cried for him to stop just as Mama was screaming for him to stop. He struck her with his fist as though he were fighting a man, and Mama never raised her hand to strike him back, except once that I recall.

He was quite drunk on this particular night and, as usual, came in to do harm to whomever was still in the unfinished house. As he grabbed Mama and tried to push her out the back door and down the steep stairs, Mama was able to maneuver him so that Daddy was the one who fell through the open door and down the stairs, unfortunately landing in a tire and passing out for the rest of the night. We kept checking to make sure he was still out cold in the tire because we knew that once he awakened, there would be hell to pay.

Daddy had light skin and curly-straight hair, and he grinned often. We, i.e. his children, smile a lot ourselves, but we cannot say for certain whether we inherited our very comfortable ability to smile (most of the time) from him or from Mama. She also smiled quite often. Daddy had a very sunny disposition for everyone except his wife and children. We were scared to death of him.

The money Daddy made during the week was spent on beer and cigarettes Fridays and Saturdays. He would sober up on Sunday so he could go to work Monday and do it all over again. Before running away to Boston, sometimes Mama would take substitute teaching jobs at the local schools to feed us. We didn't know it at the time, but the very kind lady who suggested to the principal that he should give Mama these substitute teaching assignments would become one of my in-laws. I married the grandson who she raised.

Mama and my older brothers had learned to leave the

house on Fridays, before Daddy came home, but that left Olivia, Matthew, David, Charlotte, and me to bear the brunt of his abuse. We could see Daddy staggering over the hill on his way home to beat us, and on this particular Friday evening, with the sun going down just behind him, the five of us saw him in time to run across the street and up the muddy red dirt hill, heading to Great Aunt Daisy's house for safety. Aunt Daisy and her daughter Betty used to babysit David and Charlotte when Mama had work. Matthew and Olivia made it up the hill and didn't look back. In my effort to help David and Charlotte get away by pushing those two little kids up the hill, I didn't make it.

"Gusta," Daddy bellowed. He had named me Augusta after the city where his company was building a college in Georgia. I absolutely hated it but was stuck with that god-awful name until he died. However, Mama always called me Marshall. Daddy caught me by the ankle and pulled me back down that muddy hill. David and Charlotte, holding hands, looked at me with tears streaming down their dirty little faces.

Daddy pulled me back across the street to the house that had no running water or electricity, just a wood/coal burning stove. He got a switch and took me into the house, where he beat me and beat me—and when he saw that a big lump had come up on the back of my right leg, he kept beating me in the same spot until it burst. Even though I cried and screamed and tried to pull away as he held me by one hand and beat me with the switch in the other hand, I felt nothing. From the first strike, I felt absolutely nothing, but even at age six, I knew it was better to pretend it was hurting—or he would never stop. That was my first experience with knowing that there is a God. I still believe today that God took those licks and that beating for me.

I've always loved the "Footprints in the Sand" poem (onlythebible.com) because it reminds us that when we are struggling and need God, we may think we are alone because we see only one set of footprints—but that is when our Lord is carrying us. The poem's words are a reminder of the trauma of that fateful day, and I still find it so reassuring and comforting every time I feel alone with no one to help me.

Despite all the physical abuse, I was not sexually abused as I had heard happened in other dysfunctional families. So often, it seems that emotional and physical abuse are part and parcel with sexual abuse. I am so thankful that Daddy never molested me or anyone else in our family. Even though I was afraid all the time, I was never afraid that he would touch me in *that* way, only that he would beat me to death.

After Daddy was too tired to beat me anymore, he made me fix him a dinner. Imagine a six-year-old frying pork chops and making something with the Ritz crackers and pork and beans he had brought home. Daddy said they had better be done right—I was scared to death while seasoning and frying those pork chops. I warmed a can of pork and beans to go with them, and in my first foray into conjuring up a dish, I crumbled those Ritz crackers into the beans and added yellow mustard, his favorite condiment after Texas Pete hot sauce. By the time I had finished cooking, which required starting and stoking and re-stoking the fire, Daddy had fallen into his usual weekend drunken slumber. I was so afraid that he would beat me again if his food got cold that I bravely poked him to awaken him to eat. He ate every bit, not uttering a single "Thank you," nor did he smile or shake his head in appreciation. By now, my four younger siblings who had gotten away had sneaked back to the dark house to see how I was doing. I handed them their plates and we sat on the back steps eating quietly. We hadn't had a meal in a long time. After I showed them my bruises, we cried quietly together and talked about how things were going to be so much better when we grew up.

But we would have about three more years of this hell before things would get better.

When I went to school that following Monday, Mrs. Martinez asked me how I got such terrible bruises on the backs of my legs. I told her I fell. Of course, she knew those injuries would have been next to impossible to sustain in a fall, but she didn't care. I protected my dad because the evil you know is better than the evil you don't know, right?

That very day, the same Mrs. Martinez wouldn't let me go to the bathroom and I wet myself. As the warm urine streamed down my legs and into my worn shoes, tears poured down my face. I was so embarrassed as the other kids looked on. My classmates, Quinn and Ann, looked as though they felt so sorry for me. Many of the other kids started to snicker and laugh. Instead of cleaning me up, Mrs. Martinez said, "I want you to wipe it up, and then stand by the radiator during recess and dry your dress, socks, shoes, and underwear." Afraid to say anything, I did as my teacher instructed me. I walked to the bathroom that Mrs. Martinez wouldn't let me use earlier and got paper towels from the metal dispenser there. I dried my legs and soaked the puddles that had pooled in my shoes, making them squeak. Then I stood against the radiator to dry my clothes. The rank smell of urine accosted my nostrils. She didn't care that my brothers, sister, and I never had lunch and that they never gave us a free meal. Nobody helped or cared, except Quinn, one of my classmates, who used to share her peanut butter and jelly sandwiches with me. Another classmate, Ann, would occasionally give me an apple, a banana, or an orange. Their gestures of kindness gave me such hope and helped assuage my hunger pains. The other kids didn't play with us, so we would sit on the swings away from them and eat together. When the bell rang at close of recess, we would quietly go back inside the classroom. Even at that age, Quinn, Ann, and I felt different, alone, and ostracized.

When Mama came home from one of her trips, she found out about the wetting incident. She sent a note through my big sister Emma to Mrs. Martinez to let her know that she would not allow her to mistreat me as she had done my sister Olivia, and that she would file charges against her if she tried. Mama specifically cautioned Emma to bring the note back home to her because the authorities might perceive it as a threat. Mrs. Martinez had the temerity to shed a few tears, claiming innocence of any wrongdoing or abuse, but Emma snatched the note from her to bring back to Mama as instructed. From that day on until the end of the school year, Mrs. Martinez treated me much better. She even cast me in the school play with the other children. Mama was somehow able to buy me the colorful romper that was required to participate in the play.

As I progressed through the second grade, things grew worse. Mrs. Gleason, my teacher, seemed to resent me because I was very good at arithmetic. I was so good that I was solving problems at the high school level, far higher than Mrs. Gleason had shown us how to solve. One day she noticed I was doing algebra, which she hadn't taught us. She pulled me roughly by the arm to her desk, holding me painfully tight, and admonished me for doing algebra without guidance. I stood confused and hurt. I had always been pushed to be good at arithmetic, but my teacher was telling me to stop working ahead. She was so angry when I asked her to show me how to do algebra that I wondered if she didn't know how herself. After that day, she often kept me in class during recess, grading the other kids' work. Instead of going outside, I would sit at my desk in silence, doing my teacher's work.

I wasn't the only victim of Mrs. Gleason's anger. On some days, Mrs. Gleason would force us to line up along the concrete wall of the school. Then she would choose a girl in our class to beat us one by one. One day I was hit so hard in the back that I fell to the ground with the wind knocked out of me. My hands hit the rough ground hard as I tried to catch my breath. Mrs. Gleason shouted at the girl. She seemed scared that I had been hurt worse than she intended. From then on, she said I was not allowed to participate anymore. None of the other teachers nor the principal seemed to know or care that this happened, and Mrs. Gleason continued to line us up throughout the year.

Then I had a kind third-grade teacher, Mrs. Hess. Although she did nothing to help us survive in terms of food or clothing, she did appreciate that I was smart and I was always in the #1 desk. She would even take me to the sixth and seventh grade classes, where many of my cousins were, in order to show them how to solve problems and construct proper sentences. Mrs. Hess would hold my hand as she walked with me down the dark checkerboard hall with blocks on each side. The lights were always flickering, threatening to go out. She positioned me at the chalkboard, where she would give me problems to solve and verbs to conjugate in front of the class. She would say things like, "Pay attention to how Marshall forms her letters and numbers," and, "Watch how she changes the verb to agree with the subject." She made me feel so proud and always thanked me and told me how smart I was, often comparing me to my big sister Emma.

My fourth-grade teacher, Mrs. Hunter, treated me in a similar fashion, highlighting how smart I was, but added a ridiculous component—hair length. My classmate Veronica and I were the only true competitors. I always won that one too, even though I didn't own a comb or brush. We used our fingers to "comb" our hair. We didn't have bar soap, shampoo, or conditioner. I didn't even know that there were such things as conditioners or lotions.

FAMILY MATTERS

You would think that with as many aunts and uncles as we had in the same neighborhood, they would have cared enough to bring us a loaf of bread and a jar of peanut butter or jelly . . . but they didn't. Many had children of similar ages and might have shared a coat or an outfit or two. They would drive by in their fancy new cars and act as though we did not exist. The children behaved like their parents and treated us like crap in school and out. They knew what the nine of us were going through at home, but brought not so much as a bag of groceries or a dollar to help us. The only way we received any spiritual instruction was a kind older single woman who would pick us up on Sunday mornings for Sunday school and church and return us after she had completed her duties as pianist/organist. Many of our close relatives attended the same Episcopal church and lived within a five-mile radius of our shack. May God forgive them *for what they did not do.*

A young child doesn't wonder why things are the way they are—cold, hungry, dark, scary. I had no idea that there was supposed to be something more or different. I vaguely remembered that my grandmother, my father's mother, always had hot food and lights and warmth, but she died when I was five. At that point, I had never met Mama's mom. The first time that I remember seeing her was when I was nine.

Mama's Desperate Move to
the Safety of Grandma's

There were two traumatic events that forced Mama to leave Daddy for good: First, Daddy dumped the food that Mama had just bought for us with her hard-earned money from her work in Boston in the sandy dirt. All the pork chops, ham, bologna, chicken, hamburger, bacon, grits, dried beans, dried peas, meal, flour, crackers, chips, and eggs broken, covered in grit, and ground into the dirt—although we tried to brush it off and wash it off in the pond, we could not save any of the food. Only the canned goods were left untouched.

Second, after Daddy set fire to the Samsonite suitcase that was full of her beautiful new clothes she had brought back with her from her work in Boston, Mama had finally had enough. We thought that she was finally leaving him for good. Perhaps if we had been able to save some of the smoldering fabric, Mama might have stayed.

One fall day, when I was in fourth grade, Mama secretly removed the four youngest of ten who were still in elementary school in Winston. She picked up what few things we had at the house and stole us away to live in Wesville with her mama, where Emma and the baby had been living.

Our black dog tried to get in the cab with us, but we had to leave him behind. I have no idea how he was fed because we didn't even have food for ourselves. I don't think he even had a name, because that would have made us somehow responsible for his wellbeing. He whined so pitifully as we closed the car doors and drove away that

David and I quietly cried the sixteen miles to Grandma's house. I still cry when I think about what may have happened to him.

Dad Followed Mama and Children

As I reflect on their experiences and family life during those years, based on what my older siblings shared with me, I believe that leaving Dad was Mama's attempt to start life anew, to get away from a fragile, abusive, and unpredictable life. However, somehow Dad soon managed to move in. How dare he? What nerve he had! He wasn't doing the right things for his family, far from being the model husband and father. I suspect that he didn't want Mama to "move up" and "move on" to a better life for her children and herself—not without him, anyway. Abusive people thrive on being in control, but perhaps Dad knew that his wife was finished with him, and he couldn't accept it. Funny how some people don't want to help you nor do what's right by you, yet they are readily available to hurt you and hinder you from excelling.

Mama didn't want an extravagant life. She simply wanted a life of peace, love, and respect. She wanted the necessities for her children. That was not too much to ask. His abuse didn't stop—as you would think, considering Grandma could easily witness Dad's abusive behavior—but Grandma, so I've been told, made it clear, shotgun in hand, that she would blow his brains out if he kept acting like "a fool." No one was under any illusion that Grandma was someone to play with. Even as a young child, I learned that Grandma was a force to be reckoned with.

She gave instruction once; if she had to repeat herself, it would not be spoken nicely. She had no fear and spoke her mind on any given day—to whoever was deserving of her wrath.

Mama should have felt protected, but I'm not certain if she felt comfortable with Grandma threatening her husband. Grandma didn't bother anyone and didn't allow anyone to bother her and her children. Mama had a nonviolent nature. As strange as it sounds, abused people sometimes protect their abuser. He was her husband; he was her children's dad. In those days, Mama was timid, afraid of any trouble because she had seen enough of it.

Mama certainly didn't receive consistent, *unwavering support* from her sisters and mother, and her one brother had died years before. Her father had died when she was a small child. Mama spoke about him often. She was very proud of him and felt she was more like him than her mother. Mama admired his keen interest in education. Her father was the first Black mail carrier in the county. But he had flaws she did not like talking about. Mama, based on her memories of their relationship as told to me, was undeniably a "Daddy's Girl."

I wonder if life would have been different for Mama and her children if her father had been around to put the fear of God in Dad, assuring him that it would be in his best interest not to bring harm to his daughter and grandchildren. Amazingly, when a man knows that a woman's father or any strong, no-nonsense male supporter is in her life, he seems to hesitate or think twice before causing harm to her. It's pathetic how that works—that it sometimes takes someone else to keep a man in line, to do what's right. If he really knew God and feared Him, our dad's heart would have forced him to be a decent man to his wife, a model father for his children.

Mama said that she had asked one thing of God: She'd prayed for God to remove one of them, either Dad or herself, because life was unbearable as it was. She wasn't requesting removal by death as many abused women may have prayed, but rather a separation so that the abuse would end. Mama must have been so sick and tired of being afraid and humiliated—sick and tired of being sick and tired—but God had his own plan. God always looks at the whole picture . . . the bigger picture, as some would say. I was a small child during the abusive years in our home when Dad was alive. As I reflect on the abusive life that Mama and my older siblings endured and shared with me and compare it to the better life that the younger children and I later experienced, I know God blessed us. God certainly proved that He never really left our side; He was only preparing all of us for a "new dawn," and apparently wanted Mama to be around to raise her underage children. He wanted Mama to "breathe." I'm grateful. We needed Mama. She was "the rock" we all needed. Thank God that Mama raised me, and I managed to escape most of Dad's abusive behavior.

"There hath no temptation taken you but such as is common to man: but God is faithful, who will not suffer you to be tempted above that ye are able; but will with

the temptation also make a way to escape, that ye may be able to bear it." —Corinthians 10:13

Before Mama departed for Boston to find work, she had gotten permission from Grandma to allow Emma and Goya to stay with her while Emma finished high school. Emma would be responsible for taking care of the baby after school until Mama had made enough money to come back and take care of us. My sister Emma had already been living in Wesville to help out with raising Goya, who was still only a baby. She was the most beautiful baby I had ever seen. I didn't know it then, but I would later learn that Goya was the perfect name because it means "friend." She is indeed a friend. She is a fierce protector for those she loves, and also for the innocent. Goya has never been a fence-straddler.

My older brothers had run away to live with friends some time before in an effort to escape the beatings and gain access to basic conveniences such as electricity and plumbing. They also wanted to live with a family who would feed them. I don't recall any conversations about it or any attempts to force them to come back, even though they were all under the age of fifteen when they left. I can still see my brothers walking down the road past our house carrying watermelons and bags of groceries, on their way to the family who had taken them in. The rest of us were so envious and always so hungry. They would walk right past our house without even stopping to talk, giving us a hug, or offering us anything to eat. I guess they were too embarrassed to stop at the house that had the big orange eviction notice on the front of it.

We walked to the community elementary school for the rest of my fourth-grade year, where I was laughed at and made fun of because I was the new kid entering school in the middle of a semester. I met Sarah Ann Walton, who would become my best friend, that same semester. She too was ostracized, not because she was new but because she had plenty of financial resources, was a little overweight, and looked a lot like me—really long hair and fair-skinned. In Black communities, that alone earned you the title of "Oreo"—you know, Black on the outside and white on the inside. The fact that we spoke well and were often told that we didn't sound Black didn't help.

Sarah walked me home from school almost every day, and Mama would always have something ready for us to eat. Sarah would never eat her fruit and vegetables, and I remember Mama telling her that she was going to get sick if she didn't start eating them. We didn't know then how prophetic Mama's statement would be in only a few years' time.

Things were so good at first when Mama brought us to Grandma's house in Wesville. We were so happy, clean, and warm, not scared anymore, and had enough to eat. For the first time in my life I had plenty of everything: dresses, pants, and two good pairs of shoes, one for church and one for school. Mama cooked and cleaned for white folks, and also did some substitute teaching to make ends meet. Even after she got the job as a nurse's aide at the local hospital, she still cooked and cleaned for white folks for a time.

Mama would tell me to come by on my way home from school to help her carry some of the food and clothes the white family had given her. I didn't tell Mama, but I was so ashamed and embarrassed. The son of one of the white families was in my class, and he called me nigger and made fun of me in front of the other white kids in school. It's called bullying now, but I had been bullied since first grade, so his abuse of me was par for the course. He was quite different during the days I encountered him at his house with Mama. Instead, he was really nice, fooling Mama, but the next day at school, I would be called "nigger" again and again.

TWO MORE BABIES:
JACOB FOLLOWED BY SOPHIA

Then Mama let Daddy move into Grandma's house. I think Daddy had finally been evicted for non-payment and had nowhere to go, and that's why Mama let him stay with us. Jim Walter Homes had been threatening eviction for a long time before Mama collected us from there, leaving embarrassing orange collection notices stapled to the house for all the world to see. We would be so ashamed when everyone could see it from our school bus. Daddy would just tear the notices off.

I suppose Mama thought we needed a father in the house, or perhaps she thought he had changed and would help provide financial support. I believe Daddy helped some, but he still drank a lot. The damage he had done to me during my first nine years of life was enough to keep me in constant fear even though he didn't beat us anymore once he moved in with us at Grandma's house. His loud, angry voice was enough to keep us on our heels in fear of what he might do.

Jacob was born a short time later, followed by the last of us, Baby Sophia, who was my responsibility from the day she was born. Grandma took care of her when I was in school, or Mama did when her work hours changed. Mama usually worked the 11:00 p.m.–7:00 a.m. shift as a Licensed Practical Nurse (LPN) at the local hospital so she could get us ready for school, take care of us after school, and put us to bed before she left for work.

When Mama was working, Daddy and Baby Sophia would sleep at the head of the bed while I slept at the foot of the bed. Matthew, Olivia, Charlotte, Goya, and Jacob slept on a rollaway bed. Daddy would kick me to wake me up to feed or change Baby Sophia during the night. I had to make her bottle and change her diaper in almost total darkness. One night while I was changing Baby Sophia's diaper, the diaper pin must have stuck her because she started screaming and woke up Daddy. He hit me and said I had pinched her, and even though I said I hadn't, he kept yelling at me until I admitted to the lie. I cried so hard that night, but I had to muffle my cry so he wouldn't keep kicking me.

Once it became clear to Grandma that Daddy had moved in and was staying, she locked us into the living room portion of her house. She boarded up the room and the bathroom, and our family of ten lived in that one room for a long time. What used to be our living room was now our whole house for ten people. We learned later that Mama had filed a lawsuit against Grandma to stay in the house because Grandma had tried to put us out. Mama won the case because her father had willed the house to his children, not Grandma, so Mama had the right to stay there. That was why Grandma had divided the house.

Mama's five sisters stopped speaking to us for a long time after that, and one aunt stopped giving us hand-me-down clothes. She would give Olivia and me skirt sets, coats, shoes, and dresses that her girls had outgrown; even though Olivia was the same age as her daughters, she was much smaller than they, so Olivia and I could both share their clothes. So strange that she gave us her hand-me-downs after we moved to Wesville, but gave us nothing when we lived in Winston, when we needed them the most. In fact, Mama and her sisters were never close again.

We kept that one room spotless every single day, and the beds were always made. We did have to heat water from the faucet on the side of the house and keep changing it for every two children, but we bathed every day. Although crowded, we were warm and fed. After our family of ten was relegated to one room, my duties of cooking, cleaning, and taking care of the younger ones returned and would continue until I left for college at age eighteen, in September of 1973. I was the dependable one, the one who was afraid to disappoint.

"SEPARATE BUT EQUAL" OVERTURNED

Mama wanted to make sure we received the best possible education, so in my fifth-grade year she transferred us to the previously all-white schools, Wesville Elementary and Wesville High. It was less miserable because my brothers and sister were already there, and my very best friend and her siblings had changed schools, too. But we were treated so poorly by students, teachers, and the principal—and were called "nigger" every single day.

I had a Black teacher for fifth grade and white teachers for sixth and seventh grades. My sixth-grade teacher was wonderful, protective even, but my seventh-grade teacher was blatantly racist. She called us "nigger," or "you people," and encouraged our classmates to do the same. A few students didn't participate, but they were heavily outnumbered. To this day, I can still hear her southern drawl and see her red lipstick, perfectly coiffed brown hair, wool skirt, and sweater. Even at such a young age, I wished for her to die a slow, painful, and horrible death because of how she treated me and my older brother. Matthew was suspended numerous times; then he was finally expelled when the principal had a heart attack after one of their confrontations. You see, Matthew didn't take crap from anybody. If we hadn't been so smart, and if Mama hadn't made it clear at the outset that she would take the school to court if the teachers or administrators mistreated us in any way, we would have been treated much worse—as some of the other Black kids were. Black kids were not allowed to be safety patrols until Mama stepped in and told the principal that we were going to have the same opportunity that the white kids had. Many of the Black boys were beaten with a strap even when the white boys started a fight.

Back to the prophecy, which, though false, has kept me eating my fruits and vegetables ever since. Sometime during the fifth grade, Sarah was absent from school for several days, so I stopped by her house uptown to ask about her. I was too young then to understand, but they would say things like, "She's taking a nap," or, "She's too tired to play," or, "She's not feeling well." Sarah was out sick for weeks; then months at a time; and when she finally came back to school, *I didn't recognize her!* She was using a walker, was thin, and looked very tired even though she was smiling at me. I was scared because she looked so different. She was only back at school for a few days before she was gone again. This time when I went to her house to ask her to play, her mom couldn't answer. She started to cry and the whole house seemed so sad. Sarah had three older sisters and two younger brothers. I learned later that they were moving to Pennsylvania, to be closer to Sarah's hospital. A few months after that, Sarah's sister, Rona, came by my grandmother's house and told us that Sarah had died. We were not yet twelve years old and Sarah, my best friend in the whole wide world, had died of leukemia. Her family had tried everything to try to save her, including moving the family away to be closer to her doctors, but she did not survive, and her family never returned. I think about Sarah often, even though it has been over fifty years. I named my third daughter in her memory.

I Saw Jesus for the First Time When I Was Twelve

I believe He appeared to me to tell me what was about to happen. One summer evening, we were playing volleyball over Grandma's rusted, dilapidated fence when Jesus appeared directly across the street on Mrs. Murphy's front lawn. Although her lawn was always immaculately manicured, it became even more so when Jesus appeared. The grass became greener and brighter and Jesus was wearing the brightest white robe I've ever seen before or since. His hair was brilliantly golden, and He held a staff in His hand. Everything about Him and around Him was so bright. I was so astounded at the sight that I turned and pointed and told David to look. When I turned back, He was gone. I guess He had only come for me to see, because David never saw Him and none of the others saw Him either.

A Serious Hospital Stay

Later that same summer, I awakened one morning after my birthday with a fever of over 104 degrees — hot to the touch as Mama said, delirious, and in so much pain. I probably should have told Mama weeks before that my side hurt every time I ran, but I didn't want my brothers to think I was a sissy. I was so proud that they treated me like one of them when we ran sprints or played baseball, football, or any other sport. I could take whatever they threw at me, and without wearing a glove.

When Mama came in from work, one of my brothers told her that I felt hot and they couldn't wake me up. Mama felt how hot I was and saw that I was lethargic, so she rushed me to the emergency room in the hospital where she worked. The doctor said that my appendix had ruptured and that I had to have surgery right away to remove it.

I was in the hospital for weeks but was not getting much better. The doctor released me anyway and Mama took me back home to the one room we all lived in at Grandma's house. I got sicker and my temperature soared again to over 104 degrees. Mama couldn't get an ambulance, so she asked the funeral home to take me in one of their hearses.

I had two doctors. One was really nice and friendly, always smiling and making me laugh. He would ask if I wanted something special to eat or drink and he even would put the straw to my lips to take a drink. He informed me of what was going to happen and what I might feel every step of the way in kid language while Mama was listening, always standing close by. Mama liked that he presented everything on my level. My other doctor was more matter-of-fact. He hardly ever smiled and always seemed to be in a hurry, but matter-of-fact is not what a twelve-year-old needs when they're as sick as I was. They explained the surgery—something had gone wrong with the original appendectomy, and they needed to remove a piece of something and hopefully drain the infected "blah, blah, blah" from my abdomen. I overheard them tell Mama that I had a 40–60 chance of survival. There is no doubt in my mind, and there was none in Mama's mind at the time, that the previous surgeon who had done the appendectomy had left an instrument or a sponge or something in my abdomen which would cause such an infection. As a nurse, Mama knew that something must have gone wrong in the first surgery. I never felt well and was still running a temperature over 100 degrees even when I was discharged.

The night before surgery, Daddy visited well after visiting hours. One of the nurses woke me up and asked me if he was my father because it was obvious to her that he had been drinking. I wanted so badly to say, "No, he is not"! But I was afraid that he would beat me if I ever got out of hospital. Daddy came in with a tiny Bible and stood at the window crying. I remember giving him a nervous smile, but I don't think he said anything or hugged me. At least I don't remember if he did. Who could have known that Daddy would be dead less than six months later? My whole family thought that I would be dead at the age of twelve before the new school year started, but it would be Daddy who would die in a car accident.

I saw Jesus for the second time that night after Daddy left. I had fallen asleep at some point, and so did not see or know when Daddy actually left. I woke up to see Jesus on my left hospital wall, and I got the feeling that He was telling me that He was bringing me to Him. When Mama arrived early the next morning, the day of my operation, I asked her for a doll. I had never had a doll or even asked for a doll before. I also told her that I was going to die, but that I was going to be all right. Mama cried as if she knew that I would not make it. Mama rushed out to find me a doll before surgery and brought back a white doll wearing green clothes. I thought she was the most beautiful doll I had ever seen. They let me hold her until they wheeled me into the cold operating room. Mama tried to smile through the tears running profusely down her cheeks.

When I woke up in the recovery room, Mama was still there. Mama said God must have something for me to do here. The doctors were hopeful but guarded when they told Mama that I wasn't out of the woods yet. I had twenty-three stitches from the second surgery and nineteen still left from the first. I also had a tube that ran from my nose to my stomach to drain the disgusting, gross stuff into a jar; every time the jar filled, they would have to flush the tube and sometimes change the tube that made me gag. I stayed in the hospital for a long time, until I healed enough for my favorite doctor to take out the stitches. He called them sutures and had me count them as he removed them. Unlike my teenaged hospital roommate, I survived. She had been in a car accident; she'd seemed fine when we laughed, held hands from bed to bed, and talked well into the night, but they couldn't get her temperature down. One day after returning from some test or other, the nurse wheeled me into our room and she was not there. Her bed had been stripped. I asked where she was and the nurse said she didn't make it. I was devastated. She was the nicest white person I had ever met.

I walked from the hospital wearing a green pedal-pusher outfit that matched the one worn by my doll. Mama had insurance coverage so she didn't have to pay a penny. That wasn't always the case. Back in Winston when my brother Matthew's leg had been broken by a bully, we didn't have health insurance, so Matthew had to lie on a gurney in the hallway at the hospital for almost a week.

After I was discharged, Mama hired a car to take us

back home. When we arrived at the one-room house, one of my aunts was waiting to see how sick I was. After twelve years, I'm quite certain it wasn't to make sure we were all right. She and the other relatives had had years to help us, so I am convinced that the community and church had embarrassed her into doing something to help. Her bright idea was to come and take me from Mama and my sisters and brothers so that she could talk about what a wonderful thing she was doing for her poor sick niece. This was the gossip of the time because most of our relatives knew we were living in one room and that I had been very sick. I would also need a separate bed, which was not possible in the one room at Grandma's house. I was so shocked that Mama let her take me to her house before I could even unpack my things from the hospital. I went directly from the front stoop of our one-room shack to my aunt's shiny new car. I was so sad to be leaving my brothers, sisters, and Mama, and worried about who would take care of them now that I was leaving again, but Mama thought I would heal faster if I didn't have to take care of my brothers and sisters, share a bed, or be tempted to pick up my baby sister and little brother. I cried silently for the entire sixteen miles to my aunt's house with several of my cousins in the back seat with me. We didn't have to wear seatbelts back then.

Once we arrived at my aunt's nice brick house with four bedrooms and two bathrooms, a nice kitchen, a dining room, a den/family room, and central air conditioning, she showed me the layout of the house and where I would sleep by myself for the first time that I could remember. I asked her for a glass of ice water and she said, "You know you're not used to ice water."

Her reply hurt me to my core, and it is still painful to recall. Why did she ask to bring me here if she was going to mistreat me on the first day? After that, I was afraid to ask for anything, and drank and ate whatever was put before me and dared not ask for anything more. It didn't stop there. Each morning after breakfast, she or her older daughters would set me up in the front yard under a tree by myself with a big bushel basket of some kind of beans or peas to string, snap, or shell. My aunt and her children stayed indoors. As I finished one basket, they would bring another. I don't know why I couldn't do it in the back yard, under the carport, or at the kitchen table. I guess folks driving by wouldn't have been able to see her "kindness" to me if I was sitting where I couldn't be seen.

My aunt took me back to Mama's a few weeks before the start of the new school year. She had packed some of her daughters' hand-me-downs for me. They were still in excellent condition, and I was very grateful. Compared to her silence and absence of the years before, my aunt's gifts seemed strange to me. It is so strange that for all those years we lived in Winston in abject poverty with no utilities or facilities, our aunts and uncles never once brought us a stitch of clothing, a loaf of bread, or a can of beans.

Daddy returned to his "old self," breaking his promise to me in hospital that he would stop drinking. Daddy had also promised to treat me better and that I wouldn't have to work so hard any more. He said he was going to buy us a house and we would be a happy family. During one of his drunken slumbers, my older brother Matthew, younger brother David, and I stood over Daddy with a butcher knife, fully prepared to stab him and put us all out of our misery. With every move he made, we shrank back. I wonder if he knew how ready we were to send him to the devil, who we were convinced was his maker. We chickened out, but we did manage to take $36 out of his pockets so that we could go shopping at the higher-quality local department store for the four youngest kids. David and I thought nothing about ourselves, and wanted to buy only for the little kids. We had enough to buy an outfit each for the four of them. They were elated when we came in with the shopping bag for them. Mama never even asked how we got them. I can see their little innocent faces now, but that was a long time ago.

Zoya

BORN 1962

I was born into a family of twelve children: Emma, Elijah, Benjamin, Daniel, Olivia, Matthew, Marshall, David, Charlotte, me, then Jacob and Sophia. It was common for us to tell people about ourselves based on our birth order. Our family was larger than most in our small town. So often when we were in town, in school, or even at church, people would ask, "Which one are you?" Instead of giving them our name, because our experience had been that our name was less remembered anyway, it became a habit of mine and the other younger children to introduce ourselves by chronological number. I'd answer, "I'm number ten."

The first-born, Emma, identified herself as the eldest. She always seemed to be proud to tell people she was the first-born. The last of us, Sophia, would proudly tell people, "I'm the baby."

I didn't have a horrible childhood, not even a bad one, when I think about other families' lives in my community and elsewhere in the world. But admittedly, I felt alone often in our house of many children. About six, including me and my siblings, lived together most of the time with at least one of our parents—usually four girls and two boys while I was growing up. All twelve of us were never in the house at one time because our ages spanned twenty years from oldest to youngest. The older siblings had left home already, either to live on their own or to attend college.

In an attempt to keep me safe and away from the madness, Mama sent me, an infant at the time, along with two older siblings, to a town nearby to stay with her mother. She had reason to be concerned. Grandma was okay with me staying there. She must have known from my older sister's and brother's faces that there was turmoil at home, and it could not have been hard to figure out who was causing problems.

Mama became pregnant two more times after my birth. Life didn't get any better with Dad around. My older siblings thought that he would no longer be a problem for Mama and them. However, his determination to be in Mama's life to cause more havoc was much of the same—he was still an alcoholic and obviously in mental trouble, and the messy life in a house filled with children continued. The struggle was real for Mama and my siblings for a very long time.

Mama was a nurse when the twelfth of us was born. Dad was still being difficult. Mama must have been so weary from so many years of abuse, at least fifteen to twenty. Oh yes. You might say her tenacity and strength were tested many times over.

What was God's plan for Mama? Why did she and her children have to endure so much for so long? Well . . .

Jesus, the only Son of God, certainly has taught us something about suffering. The Bible explains Jesus's suffering before and after Crucifixion. Our suffering on earth is followed by reward(s) . . . if we are obedient. Mama and each of her children, the older ones more than the younger ones, certainly experienced suffering that many would not understand—how could a parent abuse and neglect their children? As children, none of us knew God as we do now. We certainly had no idea that life would greatly improve. Later in life, we learned to trust God and his allowance for suffering. It gave us strength and our faith became strong as we believe that God loves us and anything that causes us pain will eventually become a gain as a life-long lesson. We will never be the same as before; we are strong beings who are able to share testimonies with others who are dealing with adversities as we have. We are Mama's troopers today! We are Mama's children. More importantly, we are God's children.

"Many are the afflictions of the righteous, but the LORD delivers him out of them all." —Psalm 34:19

"Beloved, do not be surprised at the fiery trial when it comes upon you to test you, as though something strange were happening to you but rejoice insofar as you share Christ's sufferings, that you may also rejoice and be glad when his glory is revealed. If you are insulted for the name of Christ, you are blessed, because the Spirit of glory and of God rests upon you. So, let none of you

suffer as a murderer or a thief or an evildoer or as a meddler. Yet if anyone suffers as a Christian, let him not be ashamed, but let him glorify God in that name."
—1 Peter 4:12-19

———————

Some of my older siblings had childhood experiences that were much more unpleasant than mine. The older siblings had to contend with Dad's abusive, volatile behavior. Some people called him an alcoholic; others said he was not an alcoholic because he only drank heavily on weekends. If alcoholism weren't such a serious disease, that observation would have almost been laughable. I cannot confirm nor deny his drinking habits because I was very young at the time. Despite not having experienced being around Dad that much because I was about five when he died, my family life was still complex to say the least. I was quite sheltered by Mama but was loved and well cared for. I can say that now, but children do not have the maturity to see it that way at the time that they're under the jurisdiction of their parents' right hand—"Do what I say because I said so." Most parents show love the best way they know how, and oftentimes they show love the way they themselves were shown.

Protecting her children was one of many ways that Mama showed her love. Her life with her family (mother, father, sisters, and brother) was far from exemplary.

I heard things in my childhood home that have "stained" my childhood memory forever: I heard conversations about other people and about my own family members that really caused me to be a timid child at times. I questioned my purpose and whether I would be okay. I remember thinking that life must be so hard as a grown-up. I heard stories about abuses of every type, including physical and substance abuse, among relatives and other people whom I met that made me wonder about my own safety and who could be trusted. I could never be anything like them. I didn't do anything to purposely offend anyone, but people I knew had and did so repeatedly. I often wondered why at the time.

Why were a few of my siblings so "rough," practicing reprehensible behavior that Mama was so opposed to when she was teaching us to be *different/better*? I thought they should have been embarrassed if people heard about their decisions, or worse, if they were to go to jail. Some incidents were not necessarily illegal but were high up on the ladder of immorality. I often asked myself, why would they behave that way . . . why were they so self-destructive? I suppose some people have an arrogance that protected their choices. Their egos were not ever on vacation. I had so many questions. Why do people hurt other people? Why do people destroy themselves? Those were grown-up questions in need of grown-up answers, but I didn't get the answers to them until much later, and the answers did not come from the people who did unthinkable things; rather, they came from people I would meet or from my own family.

I figured out some things for myself after incidents that would raise the hair on the back of anyone's neck. My journey into adulthood was profound, filled with so many life lessons. Those lessons helped shape the way I processed "life" and what the real world was like outside of the walls of my home.

As a child, I thought I could change the world. I dreamed of people being much different than what I had come to know in my own family. I often wondered: Whom do I trust? Whom do I believe? Yet I daydreamed about living a life on my own. I wanted to get married, have two children, live in a "Brady Bunch" house like the one I saw on TV in the 70s, and drive a station wagon. Even the *Brady Bunch* characters had their challenging moments, but mine made their family moments look like a cakewalk. Life cannot be like a bouquet of roses with no thorns every single day.

Before you judge me, step in my shoes and walk the life I'm living, and if you get as far as I am, just maybe you'll see how strong I really am. —Anonymous

If GOD brings you to it, HE'LL see you through it. —Anonymous

"And not only that, but we also glory in tribulations, knowing that tribulation produces perseverance; and perseverance, character; and character, hope." —Romans 5:3-4

Mama worked a lot, and sometimes she took college courses at the same time. She was a strong believer in getting an education and working hard to improve life for her children and herself. In her case, twelve children later, she was determined to complete her undergraduate degree that was delayed by starting a family after attending college for two to three years, and by a controlling husband who was far from supportive. Her life spiraled out of control after getting married. Her life was not what a young woman dreams of having. I know that's much of the reason why Mama cried. If only she had a looking glass to see what was ahead. Wouldn't all of us pay top dollar for a looking glass like that?

But Mama, despite her less-than-marital bliss, maintained an unbelievable work ethic and commitment to taking care of her younger children. When I was about five years old, my dad died after a car accident. I have little to no recollection of him or a personal father/daughter relationship that I can hold onto for whatever reason. My knowledge of Dad comes mostly from my siblings and Mama sharing their experiences with him. Their accounting of their life with him is horrifying, to say the least. There was so much verbal and physical abuse. How could a man hurt his own wife and children? I did not have the same abusive experiences as my siblings. I never wondered how I would be warm in winter or cool in summer, have adequate clothing, get enough to eat, or have clean drinking water. I wore clean clothes daily and was not mistreated in school by teachers nor at home. Our mother was a provider for her children—the way that a parent is supposed to provide for their family. Marshall's childhood, while Dad was living, was nothing short of horrific . . . so terrifying and horrific. My God! She was only a child. I hurt for my siblings for all the abuse they saw and felt.

Many people in this world can relate to that kind of abuse from a spouse or partner; children are severely scarred because of an abusive parent(s). Many family and relationship stories are untold because of embarrassment and fear. Our family did not talk to anyone about Dad's outburst of violence. My siblings probably were afraid to tell anyone. I imagine that Dad would have been furious. Mama, on the other hand, taught us to keep our life private; whatever happened at home, stayed at home. If they had talked about it or reported it to people who could have helped, perhaps the "sun" would have shone earlier. I'm grateful that the sun did eventually shine.

It takes enormous strength (for some) to stand up to abusers. It has to be done in the safest way; no one can be too safe around an abusive person. Yet God commands us not to fear or worry. The phrase "fear not" is used often in the Bible. Nonetheless, so many people, especially women, are frozen in fear.

"Don't fear, for I have redeemed you; I have called you by name; you are Mine." —Isaiah 43:1

"Do you believe God is Who He says He is? Do you believe He can do what He says He can do? Do you believe that you are a child of God with every right to come

boldly before His throne and ask for what you need or lay your burdens at His feet? You can do all things through Christ who strengthens you! And He is able to do exceedingly more than you ever imagined! Have faith today and believe." —Mark 9:23

ABUSIVE BEHAVIOR DAMAGED OUR FAMILY

To say the least, Mama didn't have a good marriage. It was a very abusive and tumultuous relationship. According to her and my older siblings, there were many fights when Dad brutally hit Mama, and also days when he came home in a drunken stupor. Based on my older siblings' accounts, he hit her so hard she'd become unconscious. My older siblings were young at the time and too afraid to help Mama. Life for Mama and my older siblings was one of constant abuse and fear of what Dad would do next to them. They dreaded his presence. How sad. How *imprisoned* and *fearful* they must have felt daily.

A few siblings told me about an incident when Dad hid behind the door in the house in Wesfield. The incident happened before Mama moved to Grandma's house in Winston. I had not yet been born. Dad had been drinking and was in one of his many volatile "fighting moods." He had already terrorized his own children but was ready to start whaling on Mama when she got home. My siblings said they were afraid for Mama and their fear left them frozen—too frozen to warn her before she crossed the threshold of hell. As soon as Mama entered the house,

Dad hit her so hard on her face with his fist, she fell to the floor. She appeared unconscious. Dad dared any of the children to help her. There was no medical attention. He wanted her to lie there. Remembering the stories I had been told over the years, her face showed signs of that harsh blow as I became old enough to recognize that there was something abnormal about the shape of one side of her face. Many years later, when I would look at Mama's face and see the scars of leftover abuse to remind her of her past life, I'd cringe in anger and sorrow simultaneously. Mama had a visible reminder of her abuser every time she looked in the mirror. I don't know why he was so angry. I don't know why there was a mean-spirited ticking clock in his head. I'm not sure if my siblings knew.

Olivia told me she hated coming home from school because she knew life at home would be more of the same . . . mean and nasty words and even hitting, with no provocation. Nothing could ever excuse abusive behavior. Each of my older siblings had the same fear and recalled the horrible things he did to them. I felt so helpless hearing my siblings' nightmare experiences. I wished that I had been born earlier. I am "the bold one," "the one who speaks her mind," "the one who will report physical abuse or any adverse behavior to police." Those are only a few of the descriptions my family has labeled me with over the years. How does a parent inflict pain on his own wife and children? I could not understand. I believe in my heart that things would have been different if I had been around to see all the meanness and ugliness that Dad displayed—and the abusive blows he released to his own children and wife—and been old enough to do something about it. No way would I have been quiet. If he had hit Mama in front of me, I would have done something about it. That is what my heart believes, and when I went to school, I would have told every adult at the school about the trouble at home, and about everything he was doing to my family. I suppose people would say *that is easier said than done.* Some people who have experienced physical abuse feel powerless to the abuser, that they have no way out of their situation.

I was not even a mist in the air when all the abuse started; I had not yet been born. It wasn't right what Dad did for so many years to our family. Cleaning up someone else's mess is not easy. Mama could not have been the same after such a horrific experience, and we were probably raised with the fear that she had grown to know from a bad man. Often, we were told not to trust people. The damage he caused is greater than even he could have ever imagined.

Mama and my siblings received little help or sympathy from aunts, uncles, grandparents, cousins, teachers, and neighbors. I was told that many of them knew and even witnessed the abuse at times—and did nothing. Unfortunately, the silence of others still exists in society today. Silence can be a monstrous killer for those who are in the middle of the madness. I call those people, who say and do nothing to help others, *co-signers.* If you know that someone is being abused and do nothing, especially when children are involved, my belief is that you are essentially and irresponsibly agreeing with the abuse or choosing to let it continue despite the tragedies that arise.

If nothing else, abuse can be reported. Perhaps the children would have been removed from the home. Perhaps Dad would have gone to jail or would have received help. A divided family may not be ideal, but living in a house of fear and horror is unacceptable. Perhaps Dad would have beaten me as he did the other children if I had been born during that time. I'll never know now. My birth order and his death protected me.

Where was God? Any reasonable person would ask the question through the anguish and confusion. Why did God allow the suffering? Did God love Mama and my siblings? Maybe I should be grateful that I was born much later—something would have had to change. Today, I could not fathom being able to watch my mother be abused over and over again. I suppose I would have asked God, "Where are you? How can you allow these things to happen?" However, I know more about God and His decisions than the younger Goya was able to comprehend. I'm fully aware that God can change a life, as my life has changed, once a person accepts Him as Lord and Savior and follow His instructions in the Bible. I'm flawed; Christians are flawed. But we are better with God than we are without Him. I never want to live a life without Him. I pray that our family story, although not a model family experience in our past, will lead more people to the Lord. He has been my (our) rock, even when we didn't feel His presence. Trust that He is there . . . always there.

Well, God didn't intercept the family dynamic until He was ready. His plan must and will prevail. Oh, but several of my siblings were different than they would have been had they not been through so much while Dad was living. A few became self-destructive themselves and sometimes abusive. I'm grateful that they are living their lives so much better today. A few also drank heavily, more than they should have, but none, to my knowledge, was as abusive as Dad was when they were children. Mama cried while Dad abused her and her children, and then the tears were shed again as she remembered the bad example left behind by her abusive husband—when she realized that a few of her children's undesirable behavior had been inherited from being witnesses of that example. As children, they saw too much. They did not have a good model to emulate. Over time, they got better, but there have been psychological damages to their families.

Thank God that He is God. Only God . . . but only God can heal. Over the years as I've strengthened my faith, I learned that suffering is a normal, necessary part of the Christian life. Suffering can be very hard to go through, and yet it has strengthened so many, including members of my family.

"And the God of all grace, who called you to his eternal glory in Christ, after you have suffered a little while, will himself restore you and make you strong, firm and steadfast." —1 Peter 5:10

"For our light and momentary troubles are achieving for us an eternal glory that far outweighs them all." —Psalm 34:19

"Therefore, since Christ suffered in his body, arm your-selves also with the same attitude, because whoever suf-fers in the body is done with sin." —1 Peter 4:1

Dad Worked Hard . . . and Drank Hard

Dad was a skilled brick mason. He made, as some say, "good money," but he didn't take care of his family with his earnings. So many times, while my older siblings told the disturbing stories over the years about their child-hoods while Dad was living, I felt helpless. The abuse was *truly felt* by Mama and the children because they sel-dom had food to eat in the house. Dad was abusive with his money, and alcoholism (or something) caused him not to care if his family ate regularly or had necessities like a warm house, clothes, shoes, food, etc. They sometimes went hungry, and usually were afraid of what he might do to them and Mama if they asked for money or any-thing they needed. They lived in fear for good reason. Living conditions were unfathomable. Despite the blows from Dad's fists to Mama's face and body, I imagine that Mama must have cried more for the welfare of her chil-dren in those days than she did for herself. The thought of her hurting sickened me as I heard my siblings talk about their experiences because each one knew about Dad's crazy way of being a dad and knew it well, whether by personal experience or hearing about it.

I wish that Mama had had a different experience. A mother worries for her children. She wants more for them, a better life than what she had, and simple conveniences would have been better than the "nothing" he gave them. I felt Mama's tears even though I was not there to see what she had gone through; I know why Mama cried.

God sees all and knows all and can change everything with a swift wave of His hand when He's ready. God always has a plan, and His plan will not fail. I trust God. I trust God because the Bible clearly states that this is what Christians should do. I also have personal experiences with Him, which I will go into in more detail in Book II of our series. If I did not have enormous faith in God, I would not have gotten through many of life's struggles. Mama taught me and my siblings to believe in God and to fervently pray. We never stopped believing in the power of prayer. We are fully aware that God sees all and knows all and can change everything in the blink of an eye.

"From heaven the LORD looks down and sees all mankind;" —*Psalm 33:13*

"Jesus replied, 'You don't understand what I am doing, but someday you will.'" —*John 13:7*

Curiosity would have people wondering, as I did, why a woman would become pregnant several more times, bringing more children into a tumultuous situation. After a few children were born, since abuse occurred regularly with no signs of ending, why were more children brought into unsafe conditions? Well, there were no birth-control methods to prevent pregnancy in those days other than abstinence; birth control pills didn't become available until 1961, and while Mama feared the man who should have been her knight in shining armor instead of being her raging attacker, a man who neglected his own children, she also loved him. I'm not an expert, but I believe it's common for abused people to love their abusers. As crazy as it sounds, I believe Mama loved Dad, but a person can only take so much before relief is sought. I recall when a few of us asked more than once if she loved Dad; she never said "No." What woman who had been knocked around, beaten, and humiliated in so many ways would refuse her husband sex and gamble with causing more problems for herself? She had to have been afraid of making him angry. She was between a rock and a hard place. I can only imagine her disgust, fear, hurt, and anticipation of a change. Yes, a change did come.

Marshall

AGE TWELVE

DAD HAD A FATAL CAR ACCIDENT IN 1968

In January, we received the blessing of our lives: Daddy had a fatal car accident. I remember that Daddy wanted to take Baby Sophia with him on a drive to Winston on an unusually cold and icy January night. Although he had placed the car seat in the brand-new car Mama had bought, Mama was able to convince him not to take the baby with him since she was sleeping and it was so cold. Daddy borrowed Jacob's hat (Jacob had a massive head for a three-year-old) and promised Mama he would bring it back the way he took it. Funny how he stayed alive and in his right mind long enough to tell Mama to give Jacob back his hat.

Had Baby Sophia been in the car, she would not have survived. The car was mangled to about a third of its size, and the car seat was crushed. We went to see where the wrecker had towed the car on our way to school, and I remember that David, Charlotte, and I were so happy to see that Daddy would have to be dead after that wreck.

We wanted to stay home from school, but Mama said we had no reason not to go. Even though Daddy survived the crash, he did not survive his massive injuries. Mama said that if he had survived, he would have been blind in one eye and paralyzed, and Daddy would not have wanted to live like that.

Daddy died later that morning, having celebrated his forty-second birthday the month before. Mama promised us that day that we would never see another hungry day. Of course, Mama laid Daddy to rest in a way *he did not earn or deserve*. She didn't want tongues wagging about how he was put away, despite the fact that he never took care of his wife and twelve children and in fact had abused and beaten Mama and us for many years. We were all in black limousines, well-groomed and well-dressed, and Daddy was buried in a beautiful bronze coffin. At the graveside, Jacob had on his special hat and coat and watched as the coffin was lowered into the ground. Yes, it was the same hat Daddy had worn the night of the accident. We were afraid Jacob would fall in, but it seems that, at age three, he was making sure it was well done. As Jacob aged, up until he reached age forty-two, he worried that he would not live beyond that age.

One of our older male first cousins (he was actually Daddy's peer as well as his drinking and car-racing buddy) came up to me to say what a good man Daddy was — and I told him in no uncertain terms, "He wasn't good to us, and nobody did anything to help us." He was quite taken aback; nearly forty years later, he remembered how angry and direct I was as a twelve-year-old. He actually recalled it to Goya thinking that he was talking to me.

We were later told that a "root" doctor had given Grandma's niece a concoction to place under the front step of the house to drive us out, praying over it that the first person who stepped over it would die or in some way be removed. Ordinarily, the first person to step over it would have been Mama, as she left for work in the evening, but this particular day, Daddy went back out after work, before Mama left for work, so he became the first person to step over the root. Evil at work. Mama was told exactly where the root had been buried; the day after the accident, we dug up the smelly root concoction, which was wrapped in a handkerchief. Grandma's niece asked Mama to return it but Mama took it to work and flushed it away. She did not want any more harm to come to anyone else.

After the burial, because we are Episcopalian, we went to repast at the church parish. I thought it was disgusting to want to eat after a funeral, so I went outside, between the church and the parish, and played with some of the other kids. I accidentally stepped on a big fat woman's foot; she actually said to me, a twelve-year-old child who had just watched her father's burial, "Wipe it off." I was so scared of this humongous person that I bent down and wiped absolutely nothing off her fat foot. Her feet always seemed to be spilling out of her shoes. I had never liked her and most of us in the church, even adults, were afraid of her because of her size and demeanor. She always seemed to be angry at something or someone. She always looked like she was mad at the world and everything in it, especially anyone who had more or looked better than she.

We returned to our one-room shack with Mama. Although the last six of us were overjoyed that Daddy was finally out of Mama's way, she seemed saddened. I guess for Mama too, the evil she knew was better than the unknown. Mama continued working, also doing private duty nursing as she pursued her bachelor's degree at the university.

Zoya

AGE FIVE

MEMORIES OF DAD'S DEATH

After Dad's fatal car accident, life became more bearable for Mama. His foot was off her neck — no more getting knocked around and fearing her husband; no more of her children being hungry; no more public embarrassment; no more of her children being exposed to a series of "craziness" — no more of him. Yet, Dad's death was not celebrated, no dancing on his coffin. His death saddened a few of my siblings. I suppose for them he was the man they knew as Dad. He was all they knew, whether he towed mean and ugliness with a strong rope or not — and a few of them took on most of his abusive characteristics. Yet, a few felt a sense of relief. Think about it — who could blame them?

I was around five when Dad died, but I remember a few incidents. The mind is amazing. It's as if it takes snapshots of things it never wants you to forget. I don't remember much about Dad's funeral. I don't remember the pomp and circumstance, all the scenarios that happen during an emotional process that comes with death, burial, and mourning. Ironically, I do remember Mama taking me and my younger sisters and brothers to the neighborhood funeral home to view Dad's body. Although I felt a sense of sadness because of the look on Mama's and the others' faces, I don't recall crying myself. I was too young to know what to feel—what the loss was. It was my first funeral. Dad lay motionless, as still as a stone, dressed up in a suit. I didn't understand death. I do remember feeling that whatever was going on, Dad was never coming back, and I remember watching Mama look at him in his casket. She didn't look relieved nor display a sense of being "finally free." She appeared to be filled with sorrow and regret for the man she married.

Dad was the youngest child in his family. By the time I was born, my paternal grandparents had already died. Mama and my older siblings knew them well. They spoke highly of my grandparents. But for some reason, and even today it's not clear to me, Dad didn't portray characteristics that his parents showed not only to their family but to the community at large. My siblings have never explained with clarity Dad's relationship with his parents. I wondered why they didn't do more about their abusive son. Where did he get the notion to hit a woman and mistreat his family if he never witnessed that behavior himself in his own parents, his own childhood? Had something happen to him as a child? Had something happened to him before he and Mama married? There had to have been "whispers" in the community about Dad. Someone knew the truth. Perhaps Mama knew the cause of Dad's mean-spirited personality . . . more than she could ever tell the youngest of her twelve children after Dad died. What would be the point? She was protecting us. We didn't have as many of the experiences of the life of horror the older ones had experienced.

Perhaps Mama knew the foundation of Dad's de-mons — why he was so mean to her and their children, yet could be kind and respectful to other people. I find that baffling, but if he could not rationalize that he was being self-destructive, how could he rationalize that his behav-ior was destructive for his family? His mind was twisted and mangled for whatever reason(s). Unfortunately, chil-dren sometimes inherit the unfavorable characteristics of their parent; for example, caring about other people more than their own family, which is sad but happened in our family. I experienced it myself. Now that I'm older and certainly wiser, I know that their behavior only reflected their personal issues and shortcomings. It cannot be in-dicative only of how a parent treated them, or how they saw their parent treat the other parent. Adults will be held accountable for their irresponsible decisions. Some people treat others poorly because they haven't resolved their own problems. Children have to forgive their par-ents in order to be free of the past and in order for God to forgive us. We were taught to forgive our transgressors. However, *forgetting is another story.*

"But if ye forgive not men their trespasses, neither will your Father forgive your trespasses." — *Matthew 6:15*

"But if you do not forgive, neither will your father who is in heaven forgive your transgressions." —Mark 11:26

"Every person should make peace with their pain, and part of that process is forgiveness." —Goya

---

I remember walking to school with my sister and brother as young children. Along the way, we'd pass a wrecker car service shop. Dad's car was still at the back of that building. One of my older brothers told us that it was the car Dad was in when the accident happened. It was all mangled and quite scary-looking for us as youngsters. We cried. It pained us knowing that he was in that car. No one could have survived such a bad wreck or if they did, their body couldn't possibly be the same as before.

We passed that car over and over again when we walked to school. After getting home from school a few afternoons, we'd ask Mama questions about Dad, the accident, and what he was like. That mangled car, the second or third car that Mama had bought because of Dad's irresponsible driving, seemed representative of many things about the family's past life. It looked how they must have felt—*mangled car, mangled life.*

MAMA STARTED MOVING ON UP

Mama told the owner of the service shop to move the car because it was disturbing for her children to see it. He did move it, but I recall that not seeing the car anymore left a void for me. That may sound strange; the wrecked car and knowing Dad had died as a result of an accident didn't feel good as a young child, but the car was "something" left of him . . . something I could see and have as a memory of Dad. I suppose I was maturing. No longer five, I was beginning to feel things. Emotions were stirring. I had so many unspoken questions that would need answers from my family, who did not always want to revisit the past.

I've been told that shortly after Dad was buried, Mama said to her children, "You'll never see another hungry day." And I can attest that we didn't, but Mama accomplished a hell of a lot more after being released from her "ball and chain." She was able to move out of Grandma's house into a brick, three-bedroom home. A sibling's service in Vietnam enabled Mama to use his military benefits to purchase a home. That was a huge lifestyle changer for us, and Mama and her children deserved it. In those days, a house like the one we lived in was middle-class living. I was about nine then. We had a washer and dryer, central heating and air, and a sizable yard. We felt rich . . . but we were not. Mama was able to make life for the last six of her children better than it had been for the older ones. It certainly was far better, although we didn't have a clue that she was experiencing financial hardships. She had a lot of catching up to do from past turmoil. She did everything to make ends meet. Despite Mama's struggle to keep a roof over our head, she surely did admirably well, considering the family history. The utility company never disconnected our electrical power. Mama really held it together for her children. She apparently made every house payment timely because we never received a threat of eviction for nonpayment. Food was always on the table at mealtime, and we had grand holiday and birthday dinners too, like we saw on TV and in magazines.

We had a life that would not have been expected from a mother who had been abused for years and had very little money. Children know they have what they need and receive some of what they want. They don't know, by their parents' creative design, that there's an ever-present struggle to maintain a decent life for the family. Only determination, hard work, faith, and prayer could get anyone through those types of circumstances. I was so proud of Mama for more reasons than one. No one should endure a life like Mama endured on their own. It's way too much, and Mama should have never dealt with what she did. The financial struggle during the early years is only part of our story, but as the saying goes, "If God brings you to it, He'll bring you through it."

———————

"Have I not commanded you? Be strong and courageous. Do not be afraid; do not be discouraged, for the Lord your God will be with you wherever you go."
—*Joshua 1:9*

"But he said to me, 'My grace is sufficient for you, for my power is made perfect in weakness.' Therefore I will boast all the more gladly about my weaknesses, so that Christ's power may rest on me. That is why, for Christ's sake, I delight in weaknesses, in insults, in

hardships, in persecutions, in difficulties. For when I
am weak, then I am strong." —2 Corinthians 12:9-10

"Not only so, but we also glory in our sufferings, because we know that suffering produces perseverance;
perseverance, character; and character, hope, and hope
does not put us to shame, because God's love has been
poured out into our hearts through the Holy Spirit, who
has been given to us." —Romans 5:3-5

"I consider that our present sufferings are not worth
comparing with the glory that will be revealed in us."
—Romans 8:18

NEVER CAN SAY GOODBYE

I discovered as a very young child that I don't like "goodbyes" unless I know I'll see the person again soon. When
I was a child, an empty feeling would come over me. I
would always feel better if I was told, "I'll be back soon."

I'm not certain of my exact age, but I do remember
when Mama told me that I was going to the Six Flags
amusement park in Atlanta. I wasn't sure why only one
other sibling, Marshall, was going and not the other three
or four children still at home. Marshall was the oldest
sister at home at the time, and I thought Mama was going with us too. Mama went with us to meet at the school
where the charter buses were waiting to drive us and
other people to the park. When Mama didn't get on the

bus, my excitement and enthusiasm left me. It was like air seeping out of a tire. Silently, I cried; I didn't want anyone to know that I was crying, but I wanted her with us. I've always wanted Mama with us (me and my siblings) ever since I can remember. I felt compassion for her even as a child. I felt that I could take care of her if she was near me—and she could protect me from anything or anyone that would bother me. I didn't know Mama's specific troubles for many years, but I knew she was worried sometimes and cried sometimes. Nevertheless, Mama waved at us after we took our seats on the bus. She looked sad in a way, maybe because she knew I was disappointed; maybe because she wished that she could have afforded to send all of us to Six Flags.

We had been riding for miles before I could snap out of it and focus on the fun time ahead. I knew no one on the bus, but Marshall knew at least one person—a girl around her age who made her angry on our return home because she tried to steal the souvenirs that Marshall had bought for us and our sisters and brothers.

That was probably one of my first experiences learning that Family Love and protection can be mightier than the Red Sea. Marshall swiftly let the girl know that she was not taking anything from us, even if it meant "whooping her ass." I was afraid, yet proud at the same time, of my big sister. We were not going home without those souvenirs, and believe me, we didn't.

Marshall

AGE THIRTEEN

"MOTHER'S SPECIAL HELPER"

When I started high school, which then was for eighth through twelfth grades, I was known as a bookworm. You could barely see my eyes above the stack of books I was always carrying. My goal was to read every single book in the library by the time I graduated high school. I accomplished that goal.

Our school had a strict dress code: skirts and dresses no more than two inches above the knees; no pants (except pantsuits); no skin showing through tops. Because of this, you couldn't come to school sporting a baby bump. Girls who got "knocked up" and had started to "show" had to go to night school. I recall only two cases during my five years in high school: one of the girls married and had to drop out of school because married students were not allowed to attend school during daylight hours. She had to go to night school. The other girl's parents kept her at home because it was such an embarrassment, with a stigma attached to both the girl and the boy. Things have certainly changed. In today's atmosphere, girls seem to see having a baby bump in high school as no big deal, even their right. Not so in Mama's house. Mama's favorite slogan was, "He made a fool out of you, but he damn sure won't make one out of me."

By ninth grade, I had tested out of my grade level and was taking classes with the upper classmen — they're now called Advanced Placement (AP) classes. As you would expect, I was not well liked, and was in fact bullied by several girls. One of them was huge compared to me and threatened me that I had better let her cheat off my tests or she would beat me after class. Thank God, one of my older first cousins was in the same class, and although we didn't talk to each other at any other time, she heard one of the exchanges on one occasion and asked me what was going on. When I told her about the threats and how scared I was every day, she beat the girl,, who was much bigger than she, and told her she had better not mess with me again. Coincidentally, at the time, that cousin was dating the man I would eventually marry less than five years later. From then on, I protected my younger cousins and others in the same way. Goya and I were always for the underdog, and we fight for them to this day.

After Daddy died, as the oldest left at home, I continued to be the person responsible for doing the cooking, bathing the younger children, and making sure they had what they needed for the next day of school. Thankfully, none of my classes posed a challenge, so I handily completed all of my homework and was always a top student. In fact, I never felt challenged in school. With so much responsibility, I often resented the fact that I was never allowed to be a child, never allowed to play. The baby had a sitter who lived on the same street so we would pick her up after school. When she was old enough to attend half-day Head Start, Grandma stepped in and made sure she got safely off the bus and prepared her lunch. One of us would go around to the back of the house to retrieve her after we got home from school.

MAMA DEALT WITH FINANCIAL STRUGGLES

Mama was still working multiple jobs, and we hardly ever saw her. She told us what we had to do, and we did it. Mama usually worked at night because she was paid a little more for the "graveyard shift." She would leave the one-room shack at about 10:00 p.m. for the ten-minute drive to the hospital. For as long as I can remember, Mama was always at least thirty minutes early to work. She always said that if you arrived on time, you were late. I remember Mama's starched white uniform (which I often ironed and starched), white panty hose, and white shoes.

Lord knows she needed every penny to take care of us—she received no Social Security payments because Daddy's employer didn't pay into the program. In order to avoid legal action, Daddy's employer had agreed to pay Mama $25 each week. As little as it seems, it made the difference between eating chicken and meatloaf each week and having no meat at all except fat bacon.

During these lean years, with Daddy's death benefits and life insurance that Mama was smart enough to carry, she was able to save enough over the next four years to buy two plots of land and build a house for us. Around that same time, when I was almost sixteen years old, our oldest sister Emma, about twenty-five, got engaged and was to be married that summer. Mama wanted the house to be finished by then so that Emma and her husband would have a decent place to stay when they came to visit. We were all so happy to have a home: central heat, running water, bedrooms, toilets, and air conditioning. We had a wall oven, washer and dryer, and beds we didn't fold up to be wheeled into a corner—oh my goodness, we had a bathtub and shower. I had never taken a shower before, nor had I ever had an actual bathtub to bathe in. Such luxuries. How had I lived for sixteen years without them?

Zoya

EFFECTS OF ABUSE LINGERED

Even when it's over, sometimes it's really not over. After Dad was gone, life became better for Mama and her children in many ways, but scars were left behind. Abuse is multifaceted. It isn't simply about getting hit or pushed around or neglected. If a person is spoken to unkindly and disrespectfully and made to feel worthless, it's also a form of abuse, and can sometimes cause even more damage than physical abuse—for some, it can be irreversible if proper counseling isn't rendered and if there is no personal relationship with God. Fear and worry are ruthless life-robbers. The victims often cannot wipe out the shameful memories, the "snapshots" of the madness, and being abused can cause a person to become an abuser. The effects of it all are so very damaging.

Abuse lived on in our family long after the "senior abuser" died. How dare he teach his children to abuse? In essence, that is the reality of it. The world did not need any more troubled people, and abusers cause trouble for others. The culprit was dead and buried, no signs of Dad to help any of his victims—his time was up. God had work to do. Healing had to begin. In general society, abusers have many faces, among them people from many professions, many personalities, and many characteristics—yes, they can even be churchgoers. They are self-destructive while they destroy others' lives—and generations are affected by their destructive, selfish, narcissistic behavior.

Mama was far from being an abuser. She didn't even like spanking us for misbehaving when we may have been deserving of discipline as children. Hitting was not something she practiced. Mama spanked me once, and she really did not want to do it that time. I remember how she looked at me after spanking me. I saw tears fill her eyes while she looked at me. I had disobeyed her, but I could tell she would have rather I had listened to her instruction. She didn't like seeing me in tears; she didn't like seeing any of her children hurting. Although Mama did not like disciplining us by hitting us, she sure did lecture a lot. Ironically, I find myself saying the same things to my children that Mama said to my siblings and me. Children often grow up to be the recorders of voices heard and actions seen.

IMAGINATION

Looking back today as an adult woman, I do have some fond memories of my childhood. When I was a child, I thought I was living a life of being too sheltered, with no freedom to be me and not enough privileges to be with friends. I felt so abnormal and inadequate at times . . . inadequate because friends/schoolmates told stories about their weekends and where they had gone to have fun. I was not able to share those stories because Mama didn't believe in having friends at the house, nor could we visit our friends and family too much. She seldom spoke of having a friend herself. *Her mantra was that people could not be trusted*—and why wouldn't that be her mantra? After all, her own mother and sisters *were not* always kind to her, and then she married a man who made her life a living hell. She told us that we had plenty of sisters and brothers to play with.

I remember how badly I wanted to have a boyfriend and date. Mama was very strict with her girls.

"Do not put your trust in princes, in human beings, who cannot save." —Psalm 146:3

"Fathers, do not exasperate your children; instead, bring them up in the training and instruction of the Lord." —Ephesians 6:4

I can recall being between the ages of seven and nine when I wanted to go play at a friend's house and stay overnight. My friend liked dolls as I did, dressing them in tiny outfits and styling their hair. I thought that it would be so much fun to play at her house. Well, Mama had another idea: "Play with your dolls at your own house with your sisters" is what I heard often. She always told me that I had enough sisters at home to play with, and I didn't need other girls to have fun. She was adamant about protecting me/us. After becoming a teenager, I remember how badly I wanted to have a boyfriend and date. Mama was very strict with her girls. A guy could rarely sit in the living room and chat for an hour or two, and going out to parties or any school activity or sporting event was very limited. I cannot tell you how left out and miserable I felt during those school days. Mama felt my pain; I saw it many times in her eyes, but she was determined to protect me in the best way she knew how. She did not want me to be hurt or make a life-changing mistake. She had been through enough for all her girls.

I think Mama was afraid that our friends' fathers would be at home and might make a pass at us or do something that would ruin our lives. Mama often talked about the behaviors and lusts of some men and how they preyed on vulnerable, young girls. However, I wanted to play with my friends so badly. Play with my sisters? But my sisters, Sophia and Charlotte, did not have the same interests I had. Sophia, "the baby" of the family, was too young, too spoiled, and stayed around Mama a lot when she was home.

Charlotte, the sister who is a few years older than I, didn't like playing with dolls like I did, so I often played alone. I usually wrote poems and imagined my life outside the confines of home. Sometimes Jacob played with me, but under the condition that he could include his large, yellow tow truck. My doll had to be one of his passengers. My imagination was fiercely creative. I imagined that I was the doll, and I could be and do anything. Great is the imagination, for it can take a child anywhere and imagine many things—and all the characters can be kind.

I had a somewhat mischievous spirit. I liked playing jokes on my siblings and making them laugh. I was often the comic at the dining room table. I would make faces and would laugh at the silliest things that easily set off my giggle box. Since I couldn't do what I wanted, such as visit friends or invite them to visit me, I became creative. I was the entertainer, and I would get Sophia, Jacob, and Charlotte in trouble for displaying bad table manners. They could not control themselves; their laughter took control, and I had no mercy on them while making silly faces. Once I knew that I had the power to tilt over their giggle boxes, I was relentless.

Mama had to be in the mood for our silly selves. If she was tired or if one of us had upset her, she had no patience for our silliness. Mama was always teaching us to behave as "ladies and gents" at all times—to carry ourselves with class so that we would display those attributes at ease while we were away from home. Her belief was that *practice would make perfect.*

"Train up a child in the way he should go, And when he is old he will not depart from it." —*Proverbs 22:6*

When Jacob was a small child, he threw a rock at me, hitting the top of my head. After seeing blood, I cried for

Mama. She ran outside to see what had happened. Jacob immediately became fearful of what would happen next. Mama examined my injury, placed a towel on my head, and told me to hold it there. She drove me to the family doctor's office; knowing Mama, she was praying that I didn't need stitches. The doctor told her to keep the wound clean and to change the gauze pad daily. While Mama drove me back home, my "wheels" started turning. I wanted to teach my brother a lesson, and I wanted my sisters and brothers to feel sorry for me and treat me "special."

My creative mind went to work. I told them that the doctor said if they touched my head, I'd die, so they basically stared at me a lot and pitied me. Oh, that was the reaction I wanted. Jacob cried because he felt he had caused me serious harm. I "milked" that emotion as long as I could until Mama blew it out of the water by telling everybody that I could go back to playing and that my wound would be healed in a few days. I was busted! I thought they would be furious about my shenanigans, but instead, they were relieved. Despite our mischief, we really loved one another.

However, on many occasions as life moved forward, *love just wasn't enough.*

Yes, I suppose one could say I was the family "jokester," but I was mainly a quiet child and a deep thinker. I imagined so many things for my life. I daydreamed often. I wanted to go places and have fun. I wish I could say I knew God then—you know, that hair-raising, spirit-filled feeling some Christians express when they talk about God. Mama introduced us to God; she took us to an Episcopal church and taught us to pray at mealtime and before going to bed. All of us were christened after birth in what felt like our own family sanctuary. Mama drove about twenty miles to church. Our church was basically a family church led by an appointed priest. We always sat in one of the first few rows. Mama believed in sitting close to the front, whether it be in a pew in church, in any classroom, on any bus, and any other place. We sang from a hymnal, knelt to pray many times throughout the hour-long service as Episcopalians do, and received the bread and juice during Holy Communion, but I was only doing those things as a ritual, something of a routine because Mama said we were supposed to. I see it now as our introduction to a Christian life. She brought us up the right way, in the church. She needed God's strength and she knew, although we didn't know it then, we would need Him too. It was many years later before I knew who God was and what He could do for me, and what I was supposed to do as a child of His. I learned so much more about Christianity. I've also learned that one can know God's expectations and still do the exact opposite. Even Christians sometimes play with the fire of self-destruction.

As many girls do, I imagined and anxiously waited for the day when I'd become a grown woman. I had a long way to go, but that didn't stop me from living my dreams through writing. I wrote letters that were never given to anyone, nor did I allow anyone to read them. They were my unofficial diary. I mostly wrote poems. Writing took me where I wanted to go. It was my comfort zone, my space of peace and self-therapy. I wish I knew where my letters and poems were now. They were my documented thoughts during good and bad times.

No Marching

I could participate in any school activity as long as it didn't require being transported after school hours. Mama worked very hard and on different shifts, and there was too much going on for her to concentrate on my safety and all that came along with me joining any extracurricular activities. I managed to convince her to allow me to try out to be a majorette in high school. I tried out and made the cut! Of course, I had to practice with the band. I didn't have my driver's license yet; besides, we had only one car in the family and Mama was usually driving it to work. I did assume everything was worked out as far as who would pick me up from school after practice.

I stayed after school for the first practice because the band director told me I had to. I loved to dance. I loved music and the marching band and couldn't wait to perform for our school during games, events, and parades in my small hometown. Plus I wanted to be with my friends. During the middle of practice, Marshall drove into the school parking lot. Mama was home resting in preparation for her work shift. I thought that it was too early for her to be picking me up, but figured she wanted to watch me practice with the band. As she got out of the car, I noticed her solemn and concerned expression. Then she dropped the hammer; she told me that I had to leave, saying, "Mama said you can't be on the band." I was not only perplexed, I was embarrassed. I told the director that I had to leave. He didn't ask many questions. I think he knew it was better not to say anything to cause me to feel worse. I was already indescribably embarrassed and near tears, but I dared not let a tear drop in front of my bandmates and the family and friends who had come to watch band members practice.

I don't remember what Marshall and I talked about on the way home because I was so disgusted, and when I got disgusted as a child, I withdrew within myself and pouted. I didn't ask many questions because I knew I didn't have the power to change it, but Mama, at some point, did say these words to me: "At least you know you could do it because you were selected," as if that were going to make me feel any better.

I was more than embarrassed, and I had to face those folks at school the next day. How could I possibly explain? If I had the nerve at that time to respond to the woman who always had the voice of no nonsense, I would have said, "What kind of rationale is that?" But those words wouldn't dare leave the safe haven of my mouth. Mama didn't look at me while issuing those confusing words. She didn't go into much detail about why I had to quit the band. I really hadn't started marching anyway . . . never had the chance to perform or march on the field at halftime during football season. No marching in the parade . . . no baton twirling for an audience . . . no cute uniform. That experience was probably one of the biggest letdowns of my childhood. Mama surely knew that I cried about it; I'm sure that Charlotte and Marshall told her that I talked about the hurt, embarrassment, and disappointment I felt. But knowing Mama, she cried for me. Her intention was not to take me through a negative experience. She felt she was making a better decision.

Now I honestly have concluded that she was protecting me in her own way; transportation was an issue and being in the band required money, money that she didn't have. Today, I call things like that a luxury. If you don't have to have something or don't have to do whatever it is that you want to do, and the money is scarce, don't press it—and Mama did not. Sometimes, she couldn't rub two nickels together to make ten cents.

Due to her extraordinary motherly skills, Mama had a way of making up for our "hurts." She would buy Little Debbie snack cakes, a box of twelve only for me, and tell me not to tell anyone about them. That's how she made me feel special; she was aware of my monstrous sweet tooth, and I suppose the snack cakes were her way of saying she was sorry that she couldn't make things happen that I wanted to do. I hid the "stress comforters" in my dresser drawer. I was careful not to open the snack cakes at any time that a sister or brother could hear the package wrap. They were mine because Mama said so. I had no intention of sharing. I earned those cakes because of my various disappointments.

My sweet tooth was fierce, as was Mama's, and sweet foods were my source of comfort, but despite the sweet tooth that Mama and several of us had, Mama taught us to eat healthily. She cooked sometimes, but because of her work and school schedules, the older sisters often cooked for us. Mama bought the groceries, and mainly Marshall served it up when Mama couldn't. We had fresh fruits and vegetables often. After Marshall left for college, Charlotte and I cooked the meals. We took pride in having dinner ready when Mama came home from work.

Mama taught us the importance of a good breakfast before starting our day. We never went to bed hungry, as she promised. We had well-rounded birthday and holiday meals like we saw on television. Mama was the provider; she made sure we had the experiences that children should have. She made memories for us. We tried to do things to make her proud, to make her smile. We could see how weary she was when she got home. I dreamed of making life easier for her.

Marshall

HIGH SCHOOL TO GRADUATION YEARS

All of a sudden, sometime between ninth and tenth grades, I became popular with the student body at large—not the popular clique quite yet, but that would follow in short order after the popular boys started drifting my way, asking to carry my books and such. I had so many suitors that I had to promise some of them that I would be their girlfriend after I finished with the current one. Of course, there was no dating in Mama's house. They were simply crushes during the school day. There was no touching allowed at the school either. Sometimes, foolish boys would put mirrors on the floor to look under our skirts and dresses, but that was as risqué as it got.

I even tried out for one of the cheerleader spots, *and I got it!* I was stunned to hear my name over the intercom among the winners the following morning after the morning prayer and the Pledge of Allegiance. The difference was that most of the cheerleaders were a bit on the wild side, and not very bright academically. Now I was in the clique. We wore the really short cheerleading outfit all day on Fridays when most of the games were played. The dress was light blue, my favorite color, with a big, dark blue *W* on the front, blue bloomers, a white Peter Pan–collar blouse, white Keds sneakers, and white socks. We traveled wherever the basketball and football teams traveled—until Mama decided I shouldn't be around such influences. You see, I stupidly told Mama about what the girls talked about on our trips on game nights. After one year, Mama made me quit.

Mama wanted us to see that we *could do these things*, i.e. win whatever we tried out for. She did the same thing with Goya, who had won a spot as a majorette. Goya was really talented at marching and twirling the baton, and she looked so good in her white outfit and tall hat, but again, Mama wanted her to know that she could win, could "own it." This time, Mama made me go pick up Goya from her practice one day and tell her that this was her last drill. Goya was heartbroken. She was the best on the squad and certainly the best-looking. Goya couldn't believe that Mama would take that away from her, but as in most things, she and I did not fight it. We turned in our uniforms. For me, it meant that my uniform would go to the runner-up, the girl whose boyfriend I had taken a few months back. She was still after him, and he must have still had the hots for her too, especially since she did things I wouldn't. So I was his daytime girlfriend and she was his nighttime girlfriend. He wanted to be seen with me in public and introduce me to his parents.

Even though we still lived in the one room at Grandma's house, she and I used to walk to town together. One day as we walked past the local hardware store, I saw the most beautiful hot-pink bicycle. It cost $67, so I asked Grandma to buy it for me. I had never owned a bicycle. She said, "You can buy it for yourself. I'll cosign a loan for you at the loan company." We went in and filled out the paperwork, and they actually let me, at sixteen years old, apply for a loan. They approved it, with payments of $7 a week.

I was so proud of myself, but when I told Mama about it, she was so disappointed in me. She said even her co-workers could not believe I would take a loan out for a bicycle because they thought I was such a responsible young lady. I was so hurt by Mama's reaction and that of her coworkers that I never once rode that beautiful bicycle. It served as a constant reminder that I had disappointed Mama. Mama expected me to behave like a responsible adult all the time, so my buying a bicycle was to her a childish thing. I *vowed to never let her down again.*

That summer, I got my driver's license at fifteen, and Mama let me take the younger kids where they needed to go for practices and events. I drove to town to pay the mortgage, pay bills, and shop for food, and I would often take the younger kids with me if they had finished their chores. Mama was determined to be moved into the new three-bedroom, two-bath house before Emma's summer wedding. *We were moving on up!* Only the bedrooms and dining room were furnished, and we had rice, tomatoes, and salad a lot, but Mama used to say, "As long as I keep this roof over our heads and the lights on, no one needs to know what goes on under it."

I was asked to run for Student Body President and Senior Class President the following year. My "best friend" and I were running for both positions, and she told me that she would vote for me if I voted for her, so we formed a pact. When the votes were tallied, she won Student Body President by one vote, which was undoubtedly my vote. I learned that day that she had voted for herself as well. It was an early lesson in politics and how diabolical some candidates could be. I told Mama when I got home that day, and she called me every kind of gullible for allowing my "so-called best friend" to make a fool out of me. My "so-called" best friend ended up on the lead float, and I was behind her in the second float as Senior Class President.

Mama opened an account for me at the fanciest ladies' store in town, where I picked out a beautiful gown. It had a Hawaiian print bodice with a forest green bottom, blue boots, and white gloves to wave at the crowd. I was a size 2, with very long hair and above-average height. Mama and my sisters and brothers thought I looked beautiful, which was all that mattered to me. Making Mama proud was everything to me, but she couldn't resist saying that I should have been on the lead float.

GOING TO COLLEGE ON A SCHOLARSHIP

My senior year was a blur of activities related to staying in the top ten and applying to colleges. Mama made no bones about it—you were not grown until you finished college and were making it on your own. As it turned out, I would be a few years late getting that bachelor's degree.

I wanted to apply to the Hampton Institute in Virginia, now called Hampton University. Mama said that

I was not going to an all-Black college because it would limit my opportunities in the future. I was heartbroken. I wanted to go to a school where everyone looked like me and no one would call me the "N" word. Mama said I was going to Colliersville College, an all women's college less than thirty minutes away from home, and I had no choice. I applied to college and was denied acceptance. The denial letter stated, "We do not accept men except as day students." This was the first time that my name, usually considered a man's name, would be used against me. There have been several more times in my life since then that the assumption was that I was a man based solely on the name. Even today, I am asked if it's my husband's name.

Eventually, I was accepted to college. All I had to do now was find the money to pay for it, so I applied for every grant and scholarship I could. I qualified for several scholarships and grants due to my high GPA, which made it so that I only had to pay for books. I was also able to get a student loan. Unlike one of the high school guidance counselors, who tried to steer me toward an all-Black non-accredited college even though I had a high GPA, the other guidance counselor actually did her job and pointed me in the direction of applying for the James F. Byrnes Foundation Scholarship.

I drove by myself to Colliersville and was interviewed by several white people on the Foundation Board early one Saturday morning. There I was, sitting at the head of a long conference table surrounded by white people, all bombarding me with questions about my life. I felt so scared and alone and hopeless. One of the men asked me a final question: "If you don't get this scholarship, how will you go to college?" I burst into tears and said, "I won't be able to go to college. I won't be able to help my sisters and brothers. I'll have to get a job and let my dreams die." I cried all the way home, driving the green Malibu with red leather interior. When Mama asked me how the interview had gone, I told her I didn't know.

A few days later, I received a letter from the foundation. I got it! Now I could buy my books and materials. I actually had about $600 left over, which I used to treat my brothers and sisters every month, and to help Mama out sometimes. The college didn't give it to me all at once, thank goodness, or I would have spent it all on them and would have had nothing left over to treat them later. The college gave me $75 each month to use as I saw fit, which went a long way back then. I also got the Pell Grant for needy students and had a job in the Registrar's Office. In my mind, I had lots of money to help out at home.

Almost every Friday, Mama would pick me (and my laundry) up from college and take me home. My brothers and sisters were always excited to see me, and I always had bought something for them. If I went out on a date, he knew he had to buy extra burgers, fries, and shakes for them too. I never showed up without treats for them.

Since I had tested out of freshman math, English, and Spanish over the summer after high school, I entered college with a reputation. My older cousins already attending the college had been told that I had "exempted out" of a number of courses and had almost "exempted out" of several more. I must say that I found college so easy that I was disappointed I wouldn't be challenged. Without even trying, I did well in every subject except trigonometry, a course in my early major of math. After receiving a "C" on a final exam, I determined that perhaps math shouldn't be my major after all. I quickly switched to Spanish the following semester.

I loved so much about being away at school, but I missed being with my brothers and sisters every day, and calling was long-distance, so I could only talk with them when I saw them on weekends or when Mama let them stay with me at the college. Of course, this was against the rules, but Sophie, seven; Goya, eleven; and Jacob, nine, knew that they were supposed to keep quiet and stay in my dormitory room. I learned later from Goya that Jacob would sneak out into the hallway and go to the snack machines after I left for a date. I would always ask them what they wanted me to bring them back — they almost always wanted food from The Shrimper or Western Sizzlin', their two favorite restaurants, which were located about eight miles away from campus. I loved to see their happy little faces when I produced their meals, even though sometimes I had to wake them up to eat it.

I went home for the summer and spent that time working for a State Government office in the capital, making more than twice what I had ever made before. With my first check, I was able to pay for David to go to summer school so that he could graduate high school early and start college that fall.

It was such a bad and sad time for the family that summer, as so much and so many of us would change after that summer. Little did I know that my life would change even more by the summer of my sophomore year, which would necessarily change the lives of those younger than I because of the mess I would make of mine.

PREGNANCY CHANGED MY LIFE IN MY SOPHOMORE YEAR

I had gone from *a promising young Black woman with a political future* to a statistic: *another poor, pregnant, Black teenager who had gone from hopeful to hopeless.* How could I now possibly fulfill my dreams, my siblings' dreams for me, and Mama's dreams?

I was scared to death, and so I went several times to have an abortion before I would ever tell Mama or Roger, the father, who was at a military college and could not marry while still a cadet. My political science professor, who had such grandiose plans for me, his star student, asked me if I thought I was the only student who ever got pregnant at the college? He was ready to help, to do whatever it would take to keep my promising future a possibility.

I finally told Roger I was pregnant and that I planned to have an abortion, but he said that if I did, he and I were over. At that time, he did not offer to marry me. What he did say, after I told him what Mama would do when she found out, was, "I guess we could get married." Not once did he ask, "Will you marry me?" I jumped out of his old, dark blue car and ran back up to my dormitory room, tears streaming down my face.

Roger finally called to check on me and to say that we could get married in May, after his graduation. May would make it too late for me to have a legal abortion, so I lived in fear until we were married by a justice of the peace on my birthday, more than two weeks after he graduated. Before then, however, I had to trick Mama and Emma into believing that we were married in February by getting a license to marry and going to a justice of the peace in another city. When I told them I was pregnant, at the same time, I told them we were married and showed them the license, the same document as the certificate except signed and notarized. Thank God, Mama and Emma didn't know the difference, but until the day of my birthday, when Roger deigned to take me to the justice of the peace to marry me, I lived in constant fear that he would not, in fact, marry me and I would have to have his child out of wedlock. During this period, I made trips to the abortion clinic twice, but I could not go through with it. Since Roger had graduated college a full two weeks prior, he could have put me out of my misery two weeks sooner, but he did not.

My wedding day was one of the saddest days of my life. Here I was, four months pregnant, wearing white polyester maternity pants and a watermelon-patterned maternity top made by Roger's aunt, waiting for a justice of the peace to enter us into Holy Matrimony. What a joke! Roger used his class ring to marry me, which he wanted back immediately after leaving the judge's chambers. It would be ten years before he would place another wedding band on my finger. He said the reason he had not before then was because he was waiting to see if the marriage would last. *What a jokester!*

There I was, only twenty, pregnant, sort of "secretly" married to a man I hardly knew—and I had to drop out of college and move with him far away to a military base. None of this was in my plans.

Now Roger had to find a job and a place for us to live until he was commissioned into the service, which would not be until October. We hoped against hope that the baby would not be born before that date. More on that later . . .

Zoya

Family Matters

There were pros and cons to being a member of a large family, but there was never a dull moment. During my teen years, I was able to wear Marshall and Charlotte's clothes, and I could "borrow" whatever they had. I loved stylish clothes and shoes. Marshall, who's seven years older, didn't have a hissy fit if I wore her clothes, but my sister Charlotte, who is two years older, would become furious when she found out that I had worn her clothes without her permission. Charlotte had a pair of caramel, leather loafers, and the tassels made them extra sharp. I liked them so much that I did the unthinkable. One night before school, I kept looking at those shoes (Charlotte's favorite shoes at the time, might I add), planning to wear them to school the next day — but I didn't know how I could pull off wearing them without her catching me. Given that we attended the same high school and rode the same school bus, I was truly gambling with successfully pulling it off.

The next morning came. I strategically got ready for school first. Once I had finished washing up, brushing my teeth, and combing my hair, Charlotte came in the bathroom. I hurriedly went back to the bedroom we shared and dressed and put on her beautiful, leather shoes in such a rich-looking color. Since we rode the same school bus, I had to really time myself walking out of the house wearing her shoes. I heard the sound of the bus coming up the hill. I walked out of the house ahead of Charlotte. She came moments behind me and spotted her shoes on my feet. She shouted, "What are you doing with my shoes?" I looked back at her and said, "I won't mess them up." She shouted back, "Take off my shoes!" I knew that since the bus driver was waiting and he wouldn't be able to wait for me to go back down the dirt road to the house, I had to keep going. I really had no intentions of turning back from my plan to be fashionable in those gorgeous loafers. I got on the bus and took my seat. Charlotte got on the bus, and I was a little fearful about what she might say in front of the other kids on the bus, but I also knew that Mama had trained us well about not acting foolishly in public places. She'd say, "Keep our family business out of the streets." That was on my side.

Family business stayed as family business, but I got a mean look from my sister. I felt she would get me later. I knew that I was going to suffer her wrath once we got back home, but in fact, I felt the consequence long before getting back home. Yes, those loafers looked very nice on my feet, with my nicely pressed slacks and crisp, floral blouse, but I never really felt comfortable. All day, I thought how I had upset my sister about "her shoes" . . . how I would have to hear her fussing very soon, and worse, how she would tell Mama. That alone surely was a lesson for me. My conscience got the best of me. Wearing her shoes wasn't worth the bad blood I may have caused between us.

The school day ended, and I was fearful of what my sister would do to me for wearing her shoes. Charlotte wasn't as mad at me as I had stressed about all day long. Whew! I suppose she was giving her baby sister a break. Charlotte wasn't talking to me very much at home that day, which was the worst feeling. I'd rather endure the tongue-lashing than get the silent treatment, but thankfully, passing time helped fade the whole "not worth it" experience. I didn't like what I caused my sister to feel that day. I felt so wrong. I didn't know it then, but God was working on my character then . . . little by little.

As with any family, we had chores, and as in many large families, at least one child was lazy or hardheaded or both. After realizing fairness was not a star in Mama's house, we had to initiate a rotation schedule for washing the dishes, cooking, and other chores, but a funny thing about rotation in our house—it seemed there was a convenient case of amnesia when it was the other person's turn to do a chore. Mama tried several different ways to keep it not only fair but uneventful, but if one of us really wanted to "sit one out," nothing was getting in the way. I never understood how Charlotte thought I would forget it was her week to wash the dishes when I had just finished my week the day before her week was to start, but I wasn't a good debater then. A comical yet timid child, as I was, couldn't be, so I lost that battle more than a few times. On her side was the fact there were no witnesses to my washing the dishes. Oh, Sophia and Jacob were sometimes home, but they didn't help the situation. They couldn't have cared less about chores and who was supposed to be cleaning. They are younger than both Charlotte and I, and they didn't have the responsibility of chores as we did. Jacob loved cooking meals for us. He would even have breakfast ready before we went to school. Mama was usually working, in school, or in her room trying to rest before her shift to go back to work. I had only one way to win the chore battle with Charlotte, and that was to tell Mama each day when she came home that I washed the dishes. Mama never had amnesia about what you told her, and she knew the personality of each of her children. She didn't have to always see the mischief to know who the culprit was. Mama called that "having eyes in the back of her head." Whomever she assigned the work to, it had better be done by her deadline.

BULLIED DURING CHILDHOOD

During my elementary, middle, and high school years, I was bullied by a few girls who attended my school. Children can be cruel. I avoided them as much as I could. Bullying is often kept silent as the victim fears more trouble or prefers to avoid the embarrassment. The bullies were careful not to bully me in front of the teachers or the principal. I never told anyone about what I was going through: pulling my ponytails, laughing at me, whispering behind my back, walking away when I came around, not wanting to sit beside me in the classroom, not including me during recess play, etc. It's a strange phenomenon that the bullied person protects the bullies, so to speak, or inherently fears what would happen if the bullying were told to anyone. The fear is that the bullying will worsen.

Children who bully usually are having a hard time themselves in some area of their life; either they are bullied at home or they are dealing with some type of insecurity or psychological imbalance. Maybe the bullies envied that I didn't do anything to get myself in trouble as they did . . . and I was popular.

I recall, while in middle school, asking my teachers to allow me to stay in class to help them get organized for their next class, clean the blackboard, or do anything that would keep me inside. Unlike the average kid in middle school, I did not look forward to going outside to play. I had already experienced girls speaking so nastily to me when all of us should have been playing. Teachers may or may not have known the reason I wanted to stay inside with them. Sometimes they agreed; sometimes they'd tell me to go outside and play. Little did they know, instead I found a safe corner around the building and stayed there until the bell rang. The other kids never knew that I was there.

One girl would meet me when I got off the school bus. Cheryl would hold up a skinny stick or her finger in my face. She said my legs were as skinny as her finger or the stick. I wanted to wear pants to school every day after she said that the first time. I told Marshall, who selected my clothes and styled my hair, that I didn't like dresses and didn't want to wear them, but she insisted and repeatedly told me that I looked "so cute in dresses." I never told her that I was being bullied—that a girl was saying bad things to me about my legs. I never told anyone until many years later that I was bullied from childhood to early high school by other girls, and even a boy once. Earnest liked me; when I ignored him, he got angry and started taunting me, and also snickered with other boys about me.

Silence is never good when being bullied. Things could get worse, but I'm not sure if anyone would have listened to me or have done anything about it. I believe Mama would have, though, which was the biggest reason I never spoke up. It would have taken an act of Congress to keep her from defending me.

I usually listened to Mama's instructions about telling her if anyone bothered me, or if a teacher was not helping me in class or doing anything questionable. But I was silent about the bullies at school. As a child, I was often silent when I should have spoken. Isn't it ironic that "silent" and "listen" are spelled with the same letters, although a person can cause controversy if there is no use of them simultaneously in favorable ways to help him or herself?

Boys liked me, even though they couldn't call or come to my house. They could only walk me to class, eat lunch with me in the cafeteria, and talk with me during breaks. That was the extent of being my boyfriend—love it or hate it. It wouldn't have made any difference to my mama. In my case, bullying was about jealousy. I was a cute girl with beautiful, long hair, and I dressed well. Admittedly, I was sort of the standoffish type because of the way Mama had taught her children to be skeptical of people. If my older sister Charlotte was around, no one bothered me. She was known to fight if she needed to. We argued at home, but while at school, she always defended me. Before Charlotte graduated, she put the word out around school that she would return if anyone bothered me. I felt empowered.

During my junior year, I became fed up with those intolerable few girls. I never bothered anybody, and one day, I blew up. I was wearing a dress, a requirement for female contestants who were participating in a high school talent competition. One of the jealous girls started following me down the hallway, taunting me. I turned around and told her that if she didn't shut her mouth that I was going to take off my dress and whip her ass. Yes, I was fed up. I had taken crap since elementary school. Mama never knew about it, and if she had known, there would have been a day that many would have never forgotten. She would have lectured everyone, from the principal on down to the girl who bullied me.

I had no more trouble after that momentous day. I learned that I had to stand up for myself. I spent all those years feeling uncomfortable and was treated unkindly . . . for no reason other than paying the price for others' insecurities. The long-term problem with bullying is that those who bullied during their childhood can grow into "adult bullies," becoming abusive to their children and/ or spouse. The girls and one boy who bullied me during my childhood in school were children of parents who were known to have suffered the same behavior when they were children. Now, those same people have negative attitudes and walk around town with sour lemon expressions. They seem to have never resolved their personal problems. The long-lasting effects can never really be measured.

"Bullying is never acceptable. Some children feel power-
less while the bullies empower themselves with hurting
others. There are warning signs to look for, but the most
important thing a child can do is report the bullying.
Fear cannot win." —Goya

"Bullying is a form of aggressive behavior in which
someone intentionally and repeatedly causes another
person injury or discomfort. Bullying can take the form
of physical contact, words or more subtle actions."
—American Psychological Association

"Bullying has everyone worried, not just the people on
its receiving end." —Kids Health

MAMA FOUND COMPANIONSHIP

A woman deserves to experience a loving, caring relationship, a relationship with someone who truly sup-
ports her and cares for her the way any woman would
appreciate. Mama did not experience that with Dad,
but after his death, a few relationships over many years
distracted her from remembering her heartaches during
her previous married life. Now, she was working hard to
make ends meet and was raising five to six children—a
good, understanding, and supporting man surely would
fit nicely, and then Mama met someone. There weren't
many eligible bachelors in our small town, but Merlyn

was nice enough. He certainly deserves credit for causing Mama to giggle while they talked on the phone and while they sat in the dining room. His voice was heavy. He smoked cigars and brought things for Mama to help her and her children, such as groceries. Merlyn even bought a pony for Jacob and a dog for us. We felt privileged to have them. None of our neighbors and friends had a pony for a pet; perhaps a dog or cat that was running around in their yard like a stray. Jacob was so happy about the pony. It was white and was easy to spook in the beginning. I suppose he had to get used to his new home . . . our house and the environment. All of us chipped in to brush and feed it and walked it around the yard. Jacob rode it occasionally. I tried but was thrown off. I didn't know that horses didn't like it when anyone tried to saddle them from behind. After a while, Mama told Merlyn to come back for the pony because we weren't maintaining our responsibilities to take care of it anymore. After the honeymoon wore off, we got preoccupied with other things. Mama surely didn't have time to care for it. Our pet dog Missy became part of our family and was much easier to take care of. That chihuahua was a fast runner, and we had so much fun with her. When she had her pups, she had enough for each of us to claim as our own. Mama made it clear that we had the responsibility to take care of Missy and her pups, and we did. We gave a few of the pups away to people whom we knew would provide a good home for them. Missy's pups were so beautiful.

Merlyn did his best to show kindness to us because he knew we didn't have a great father experience. He looked at Mama with admiration. He was shaped like

Santa Claus and laughed and smiled a lot, but he was not about the nonsense. Mama didn't allow him to discipline us. Merlyn certainly did not ever stay overnight. I didn't think anything of it at the time, but Mama really did set many positive examples. She knew that her children, particularly her daughters, were watching her. She never allowed Merlyn in her bedroom. In fact, he never went further than the dining room, where she may have served him water or coffee. He didn't have dinner with us more than once or twice over the course of many years of their dating. Mama set the standard, and he never crossed the line.

Our mama was a very dignified woman, and although she was not perfect, neither were her children; some things just didn't happen because of her respect for herself and for us. Merlyn passed away; I think it was his heart. Mama mourned but silently. She often cried when she thought we didn't notice. We missed him, and a few of us still occasionally speak about him and his contributions to our childhood. Merlyn was the man who showed us what a kind man looks like because some of my siblings had not seen too much of that.

Mama had another friend. We called him "Pole Face." Whenever children give someone a name like that, *there's no love lost.* Pole Face was bossy and demanding of Mama's time, disrespectful, and acted too old—and he was old. He was also a heavy drinker. Mama dealt with him for conversational purposes, I suppose, and those conversations were mostly on the phone. No way would he be around her children except to say *Hi* or *Bye* or for small talk. It was clear to us that she didn't like him as much as she had liked Merlyn. I think she felt sorry for "Pole Face" because he had but a few friends and the one daughter who didn't have much, if anything, to do with him. Well, Pole Face eventually passed away too.

Age Fourteen to Fifteen: Babysitting

Several summers and during school holidays, I went to West Virginia to babysit my eldest sister Emma's two children. Mama thought it was a way for me to have a vacation that she couldn't afford; perhaps it was her way of protecting me too. Emma and her family traveled a lot, especially summers. Mama knew that I would be able to travel to many places while with them.

Mama was right. Emma and her family took me with them to different places such as Virginia, Delaware, South Carolina, and Washington, DC. We visited family and their friends; since they were educators and always had a focus to not only learn but also to teach, we visited historical places such as the Washington Monument, Delaware State University, NC A&T State University, and the list gets longer. I enjoyed babysitting my niece and nephew during summer months. I felt like a grown-up. Once their parents left for work, I became the surrogate mother. I wanted to be the best aunt for them. I pretended to be a teacher and had them read to me and asked them to spell words. That experience ultimately helped me to become a "teaching mother" for my children. Spending time with my sister and her family was always about babysitting and traveling. I had to clean and help cook and even painted the inside of their house. It was not a good job, but I heard no complaints from them.

After all, Emma and her husband John were educators: my sister was a schoolteacher when I was a child, and John was a professor at a well-known university. He made great efforts to teach others about science, fishing, boating, cooking, building small projects, and so much more. He took great pride in taking us to the Observatory, a place we had never experienced before, where we could see the sky in full view in a closer way than normal. John was the surrogate father for me and the younger siblings and a loyal friend to the older ones. He was loved by all of us. Mama had respect for him and was happy that her eldest daughter had found a "good man."

I believed then and still believe today that Mama sent me to Emma and John's house to stay sometimes, even when I rebelled to stay at home with her, not only to babysit my sister's children during summers when she and John had to work but because I was complaining about not being able to go anywhere with friends. Also, I had reached an age of wanting to talk to boys, which was a definite "No-No" for our mama. She couldn't be at home every hour to monitor everything. Mama was forever trying to protect us while using every avenue to educate us and expose us to memorable life experiences. Mama may have wanted to do so many things for her children, but she had so many constraints that I'm empathetically aware of now. She had to make so many decisions related to managing her family. Now that I'm an adult, a former wife, and a mother, and have worked to provide for my children and "proudly" made sacrifices,

I know that so many decisions require *removing "self"* so that your children can have a fighting chance.

Yes, I'm aware of Mama's struggles. I know why Mama cried. God and I know that we, as her children, benefited from her loving care and life lessons in so many ways.

Mama Showed Her Love in Many Ways

On a few occasions as a child, I was able to see something I started all the way through until the end. I entered a beauty and talent contest, sponsored by my high school. Mama really made up for my disappointment of not being a majorette for my high school marching band. The contestants had to have three outfits — casual, talent routine, and formal. Mama took me to two of the most expensive stores in a city near us. Our hometown had limited clothing stores of the caliber and expectations that Mama had. She believed that if you're going to do something, do it with style. I was so happy. Mama always believed in quality, high-end stores. She always "stepped out" clean and sharp. She often said, "If you buy cheap, you'll be buying over and over again. Cheap clothing does not last. Buy quality things and you won't have to buy them again." We didn't shop all the time, but when we did, the clothes and other things she purchased were of 'top shelf' quality. Mama was proud of herself when she was able to buy things for us, unlike the years when Dad was living. She would shed tears of joy. I knew she was happy because her tears were countered by a smile on her face and a satisfied twinkle in her eye.

I practiced my dance routine for the contest at home

in my room. I never had formal dance lessons, but I had watched enough television shows that helped me to use my imagination. I had form and style as if I had had prior, formal dance training. Mama had bought expensive burgundy leotards for me. I was nervous about performing in front of an audience because I had not done it before on an auditorium scale. I had only danced in front of my siblings, which was totally different and not as scary, but Marshall helped me settle my nerves. I think it was she who first taught me not to look at any face in the audience, but to simply look out as if no one were there. It worked. I didn't win the contest that would have afforded me the name of Miss Pagion (name of our high school yearbook). As the winner, my picture would have been on the first page, and my popularity would have been through the roof. I was the first runner-up, though. I was okay with that because I received so many compliments about my outfits and my dance routine. As Marshall told me in later years, "You danced like you had taken lessons; no one knew otherwise." That made me feel like a really talented dancer, and my self-esteem went up even higher than before.

Mama wasn't satisfied with my not winning. She believed that I should have won first place. I don't recall the details of what Mama and the judge talked about — Mama approached her after the contest ended. Mama never feared anyone when it came to standing up for her children. After Dad died, she was a woman who took no prisoners. Everyone knew not to mess with her children. She said to the judge, "You know darn well my daughter should have won. She was the best one on the stage."

The judge responded carefully—thankfully so, because Mama could tongue-lash the best of them. Mama showed her love and support for me in a public way. I was so proud that she stood up for me, no matter the outcome. I knew that the decision wouldn't be reversed, but Mama was not going to leave that auditorium without making her feelings known. I definitely get that trait from her, and I've passed it on to my son and daughter. We'll never be cruel or disrespectful to anyone intentionally; we expect the same courtesy, and fair treatment is a must.

"Hearing 'I love you' is wonderful. When someone shows their love for you it is not only wonderful but gratifying and unforgettable." —Anonymous

---

Mama's Determination and Faith in God

Mama did extraordinary things in her life, with many speed bumps and potholes in the road. As a single woman she raised remarkable children overall, and she did everything she could for her children. Although we have an array of complex personalities, all of us have a strong sense of who we are, and we have always been proud that she was our mother. She endured what she did as a child (things that I won't mention) and as an adult woman during an era when not only was her personal life a shambles, but she had to fight to claim her place in society, including the world of employment.

—————————

"The steps of a man are established by the Lord, when he delights in his way; though he fall, he shall not be cast headlong, for the Lord upholds his hand."
—*Psalm 37:23-24*

—————————

Mama always reached for the stars and implored us to do the same. If we didn't succeed, it sure wasn't because we didn't have a model. She was proud of each of us, although from time to time each of us disappointed her as children will do. We all did things that Mama disliked. I didn't do well in college during my sophomore year. I was away from home and free to "hang out"—a freedom that I did not know about before. Happily, she did live to see many of us do very well. I was determined to complete my degree; in fact, I graduated summa cum laude. Our family has enough successes and journeys to fill a small library.

It's said that God gifts each of us with a talent. Well, thank you, God! Mama's children have loads of talent. Her talented and intellectual grandchildren and great-grandchildren are truly a magnificent bunch. I can attest that hard work and desire matter, but the genetic component is quite powerful. God really did give each of us a gift. It was up to us to tap into it and use it for good. Mama was a very skilled writer, which many of us are too. Some of us are great speakers, and many of us are gifted with the ability to encourage others.

_____

"For just as each of us has one body with many members, and these members do not all have the same function, so in Christ we, though many, form one body, and each member belongs to all the others. We have different gifts, according to the grace given to each of us. If your gift is prophesying, then prophesy in accordance with your faith; if it is serving, then serve; if it is teaching, then teach; if it is to encourage, then give encouragement; if it is giving, then give generously; if it is to lead, do it diligently; if it is to show mercy, do it cheerfully."
—*Romans 12:4-8*

_____

Our talents and gifts include professional positions in the fields of skilled masonry, carpentry, painting, teaching, entrepreneurship, high-echelon managing, law, medical management, and, of course, writing. Most of us are in leadership roles, impacting thousands if not millions of lives. We will have more entrepreneurs in our family, which is often encouraged, if it brings them gainful independence and peace of mind, if it serves others, and, of course, if it be the will of God.

And we are a good-looking bunch. Oh yeah! I suppose I'm not being modest here. We didn't selfishly give ourselves that label; we heard it all our lives. Mama knew it, of course, often hearing, "You have good-looking children." Yet, she would not allow us to act arrogantly because of the compliments. She taught us to be humble and told us regularly, "Pretty ain't gonna get you anywhere without something upstairs." We knew early on that meant we must study while in school and do our best in life to be the best version of ourselves—but most of all, we had better not embarrass her. As she would often say, there would be "consequences and repercussions." Mama had a way with words that made them "stick." But somehow, she also made sure our self-esteem was high up there with the stars. She didn't allow us to place anyone on a pedestal. Oh no. Everyone was equal . . . certainly not better than any of her children, and she made no bones about it, nor did she hesitate to remind anyone who needed reminding.

Mama wasn't able to attend PTA meetings and such or take us to many school events like sports games, school plays, etc. She often worked the night shift and rested during the day. However, her presence was not necessarily needed at school meetings and events, for our teachers, counselors, and principal knew where she stood concerning our wellbeing. We didn't complain to her about it too often, but Mama didn't like people visiting while she wasn't home. When she was home, she was so tired and spent time catching up with our individual needs, and all the things that were required as "head of household" were plenty for her scarce schedule. True, she didn't trust too many people. Mama trusted God. I suppose having a past of deep hurts, so many people disappointing and

betraying her, overcame her—that is more than under-
standable.

Mama talked so often about doing the right thing,
staying out of trouble, and pursuing an education that we
just about knew what her "sermon" would be if we did
anything opposite of what she taught us. Whenever we
did the opposite of what she told us, she had a disappointed and hurt look on her face that oftentimes made me
wish that I could wipe her pain away. Mama had count-
less days of disappointments. With twelve children, the
probability of disappointments was greater for her than
it would be for a parent with fewer offspring. I believe
Mama's tears were her source of strength. It seems nothing would cause her to give up on what life could be. She
never threw in the towel; rather, she used the towel (experiences) to make the next day better than the previous
one. She pursued greatness. She was not in the business
of looking back at failures; failure was Man's word, not
hers. But Mama was not made of bricks and steel; she
was still a human being made of flesh and blood. Determination and courage lived in her heart. I wish life had
been different for Mama. *I surely know why Mama cried.*

Marshall

MOVED WITH MILITARY HUSBAND ROGER AND HAD A BABY

Roger found a temporary job at a convenience store, and we spent the summer living between his friend's house, Mama's house, his aunt and uncle's house, and his grandparents' house until we received a call from the subsidized housing folks when we were offered an apartment. We also received food stamps.

Roger would take me to work with him at the store every day because an old girlfriend of his had threatened to kill both our unborn child *and* me. Roger claimed that they did not have a relationship, and that she was insane. She continued to stalk him and issue threats, but for some reason, he refused to file charges against her. Never secure in the marriage from the beginning, this potential threat served to keep me unsettled until we moved to our first assignment over 800 miles away from her.

As bad luck would have it, our daughter Lily arrived three weeks early, so we had no free healthcare. We did have Mama, who provided us with lots of advice and instructions on how to take care of our child, diapers, formula, vitamins, shampoo, lotion, diaper cream, and powder. Roger's aunt helped out a lot too, and so did his grandmother. They had cows, chickens, pigs, and crops, so we always had plenty of food to eat.

I frankly do not know what we used for money. Between the day we got married, my birthday, and the day Roger received orders, I don't remember actually having any money in my personal possession until after we received our first military relocation assignment. Roger would give me an allowance of $50 a month after that. Looking back, I cannot believe that I allowed myself to be treated in this way.

After Roger received orders, he had to go away to Officer's Training School for a while. Our daughter was about three weeks old when he left, and the last thing he told me before he left was to make sure I had the pregnancy weight off when he came back. I was so scared and insecure that I actually did get the weight off and was back down to my pre-pregnancy, twenty-year-old weight by the time he returned six weeks later—because he had threatened that he wouldn't take me with him to his first assignment. I ate nothing for six weeks. I bought fruit juices, boiled them down so that they were super sweet, and drank the hot, sweet liquid three times a day for my meals. I did 100 sit-ups and 100 leg lifts every day. I did not want him to leave me behind; not because I wanted to leave my brothers and sisters but because I thought I would be able to help them more and maybe even bring them to live with us. How naïve was I to think that my shotgun marriage would be strong enough to support taking care of my brothers and sisters.

When Roger returned from training, he seemed pleased that I had lost so much weight in such a short period of time. He had to pack up and head to his new assignment. Once there, his plan was to find us an apartment and send for us. The transportation personnel sent orders for the movers to pack my things, and I received our flight information. It was yet another sad day when his aunt picked the baby and me up from Mama's house to take us to the airport. Neither Mama nor any of my brothers and sisters were home to see us off. Mama was working and my sisters and brothers were at school or in college. Roger's aunt, always critical of my family as "city folk," made fun of how the baby and I were dressed because it was pretty cold that December day in 1975. The baby didn't even have a hat on, and I had only a light blanket covering her head. I had sent almost everything on ahead with the movers. If Mama had been there, she would have made sure the baby was properly covered. Mama had a soft spot for this baby and knew how to hold her to stop her crying.

Roger was waiting at the airport when we arrived. I was scared to death. I was 800 miles away from home, *and I was going to have to live with this man!* When we arrived at an apartment building, we walked up the stairs to the second floor. When we entered the apartment, it was completely furnished so I asked whose place it was. Roger said it was ours, and that he had bought all the furniture for the one-bedroom apartment (bed, dressers, bassinet, kitchen supplies).

Over the years, Roger did that a lot. I think it was his way of letting me know that he was in control—that I was powerless. I stayed in the apartment all day because I knew no one, and was afraid to venture out without him. I would cook whatever he bought. He took the car every morning, so even if I wanted to go somewhere, I could not. I decided that what I needed was another baby for me—and the child I already had. When the baby was about four months old, I became pregnant with our second child.

We moved into military housing before our second child was born. In early 1976, there was an investigation into why Black families were not being assigned housing in certain coveted areas of the base, and since we were next on the list for family housing, we, as second lieutenants, were quickly moved to an area where previously only white lieutenant colonels and above were assigned.

Some of the other Black officers' wives were jealous and wanted to know who we knew to have gotten such a plum housing assignment. The house was so large that we could not furnish it all. We had very few kitchen essentials, no formal or informal dining room furniture, no nursery furniture, and no second, third, or fourth bedroom furniture. These areas remained unfurnished. We didn't have a telephone or a washer and dryer. Roger would take me to the laundromat after he got back from work one night each week and leave me there until I was finished. I would be so scared but for a time, I didn't think I had a choice because I had to wash my baby's things.

I finally got the nerve to get a job at a local hospital, working at night as a nurse's aid, just like Mama. By working the graveyard shift, I could use the car without interfering with Roger's work schedule or his semiprofessional baseball schedule. My work schedule was 11:00 p.m. to 7:00 a.m. I was home in time for him to leave for work at 7:30 a.m. My plan was to work for three months, long enough to buy a washer and dryer before my due date. As it happened, that's all I needed to be able to buy the washer and dryer, a crib for the first daughter, a play-pen for the new baby, and a dresser with a changing table to house their things.

On my last night as a nurse's aid, one of the patients who was always on my roster to care for died of lung cancer. Her daughter treated me as though I needed the care, not her and her dying mother. While I stood frozen, screaming and crying for help as her mother was throw-ing up so much blood and tissue, her daughter came to me and hugged me. With her mother's blood splattered all over my white uniform and white nurse's shoes, she was comforting me, telling me it was going to be all right.

At the time, I thought it was so strange that the daugh-ter was comforting me after we both witnessed her moth-er vomiting her lungs out, but since I made Jesus my Lord and Savior, it is now quite clear. They could see then what I did not until much later—that I was a Child of the Most High God. They could feel that there was something about me they needed to embrace.

I was also in nursing school at the same time because I wanted to do what Mama did. There I was, once again a pregnant student. The nursing school had strict rules about attendance, so I had to continue going to my class-es and doing the practicum part of the nursing school curriculum at nursing homes and hospitals even when I was nine months pregnant. One of the other officers' wives and I had become friends, and she kept the girls for me while I attended classes.

Our second daughter, Claire, was born a scant thirteen months after our first daughter. Almost immediately following her birth, the marriage went from bad to worse. It went downhill so fast that I could not stop it. I tried everything to try to keep the marriage together because I wanted the girls to have both of their parents in the home. Roger drank a lot, and when I confronted him about it and the fact that there was no food but plenty of his liquor, he said that his gin and mixers came first. I was hurt beyond words.

How many ways does a husband have to tell a wife that *he doesn't give a damn?*

I dropped out of nursing school and became really depressed. Once again, I had failed to finish my degree. I saw myself as an abject failure in everything except being a mother.

Looking back, I probably had post-partum depression, but what self-respecting Black mother would admit that during the 70s? A few years later when I was back at college to finish my degree, I told my psychology professor how my husband made me feel, and he told me something that I have never forgotten, "That's not how he makes you feel. It's how you allow him to make you feel." I became empowered that day by those words, and I knew then that the Lord placed me there to hear those words. Never again would I allow Roger to make me feel small or less than anything or anyone.

It seemed that Roger tried to be away from home until late, yet he expected me to get up and feed the girls when they awakened during the night. I would not. While he was easily disturbed by any sound, the noise of a baby's cry did not bother me. I heard it throughout the day and so, when they cried during the night, Roger would tell me to go get them, but I stood my ground. I told him I would not because I had them all day and most weekends by myself, so while he tossed and turned trying to ignore the cries, I would snap my fingers in time to their "musical" crying. Eventually, he could stand it no longer and would get up and feed and change them. Roger tried to have the same "hands-off" behavior when it came to doing the laundry, cooking, and dishwashing. One week we had used every dish, pot, pan, cup, and glass—and neither of us gave in to doing the dishes. Once he figured out that I was doing nothing without his doing his share, I would wash the dishes and he would rinse them.

Roger drove the car to his work every day, whether or not the girls had pediatric or dental appointments. We did not have a stroller, so I would walk the distance to the hospital with a child on each hip. Even when he didn't need the car, he would drive it and leave it somewhere else so that I was still left without transportation.

I was at rock bottom emotionally when I told Roger one evening that if he didn't give me the money to leave, l would kill myself. For a man who never had any money when I asked, he came up with enough for my two children and me to take a flight out of Hebron and move to Shiloh. I had planned to move in with my old childcare provider and her daughter while her husband was overseas, and then find a job. Roger gave me $100 for us to live on and said he would send me $100 a month. We lived on hot dogs and corn for the three weeks we were there. It seemed even longer than that; I couldn't stand it anymore. Contrary to what the woman had told me before, the room she offered us had only a cot in the second bedroom. The cot was too small for even one of the children or me, so my two-year-old slept on the cot and I slept on the hard cement floor on a blanket beneath her with the baby on top of me so that she would be comfortable. It was the most difficult three weeks of my motherhood. I finally called Roger's grandmother, Mama Hildy, and asked if we could live with her. She told me I should go home, and that she too had endured a lot in her marriage.

I did go home—to Mama. When she picked me up from the airport with my children in tow, she told me that she would give me a car, and since by now Roger had orders to go overseas, I could stay with her and my siblings until his assignment was over. Mama told me that I should finish my degree while he was away. She said that if I did not get it while he was gone, I never would. Now age twenty-four, I was re-admitted to the same college I had started when I was eighteen years old.

As was customary back then, once a member was sent overseas, they could have their choice of follow-on assignment locations. Roger chose a military base in his home state. We lived at Mama's for the thirteen months that Roger was overseas. Thanks to Mama and my two sisters, Goya and Sophia, who had babysitting duties for Lily and Claire, I was able to complete my last two years of college during that time by taking the maximum number of hours each semester and during the summer. Mama was attending the same college, pursuing her degree in

Early Childhood Education. We had several classes together and studied together most evenings even though she had to work the graveyard shift at night. I remember Mama almost falling asleep in class sometimes, but we both persevered. Before exams, I would test Mama and she would do the same for me. We had so much fun as mother and daughter taking some of the same classes. I couldn't wait to see her sitting at her desk as I entered the class. Mama was always early because she would be getting off work at 7:00 a.m. and I was always rushing because I had to get the girls ready and then drive the thirty minutes to attend my classes.

Charlotte was also a student there during the same period, and the three of us had a class together. Mama graduated with her bachelor's degree in May of 1982. My initial graduation date would have been May of 1977; instead it was August of 1980, three years later and with a husband and two young daughters. Roger had returned in time to see me receive my bachelor's degree in Psychology, but I only cared that Mama saw me graduate from college, something she wanted for all of us. Emma and her husband were there too. Others thought that I should be so proud, but I only cared that Mama was proud. Had she not pushed me, I don't believe I would ever have gotten my degree.

"Sometimes in life we have the will, but we can't find the way. At other times, we know the way, but we can't seem to muster the will." —Etta James

---

Right before Roger returned from overseas in Korea, he was sent a letter from a woman. It was addressed to his new assignment squadron, but since the unit did not know he would be assigned there very soon, they forwarded his mail to my stateside address. Of course, I opened it, but because it was written in Korean, I could not read it. I did have a friend from college who was fluent in the language, so I asked her to translate it for me. After reading it, she told me she would not tell me what it said because it would hurt me. She did say that Roger had been unfaithful to me while he was overseas. When Roger returned, I showed him the letter and asked who the woman was. He claimed she was a poor Amerasian who he helped out while he was over there by buying her such things as soap, shampoo, conditioner, deodorant, and detergent. He tried repeatedly to take the letter from my hands, but I would not let him have it. I held onto the letter for months, but at some point he must have found it because I never saw it again. If the relationship had been as innocent as he claimed, why did he need to have the letter?

Throughout my suffering, I never felt that I could tell Mama and Emma how Roger was treating me. Because of his grandmother, Mama Hildy, they thought he had the right pedigree for our family, and I was convinced that they were right. I should have been more focused on our spiritual pedigree: a member of the Royal Family of the King of Kings and Lord of Lords.

I can honestly say that next to Mama and her belief in God, Mama Hildy was the most Christian-like, Bible-believing person I have ever known. No wonder she and Mama cared so much for each other. Their character and integrity drew them together. Mama believed that "the apple doesn't fall far from the tree," so she thought Roger would be a lot like his grandmother. Mama was right that Roger would be a good father and provider, certainly better than the one I grew up knowing. He provided food and shelter and love as he saw fit to give it, but he did not know how to love me, a broken girl with so much pain and insecurity still inside.

At the time, I thought that if I was the perfect mother and wife to him and the girls, Roger would be able to fix broken me. It was many years later that I finally learned that only I could fix me and only with a relationship with God, growing in Him. Mama always told us

that God (not time) could heal all wounds, but I couldn't see how that was going to work. Even though I went to church, tithed, shared all that I could for charitable causes as well as Mama and my sisters and brothers, took my children to church, and for a while convinced Roger to join us, I felt so small that I thought I could fit on the head of a safety pin. I should have believed in the Lord Jesus Christ, and drawn strength from God's word:

"He heals the brokenhearted and binds up their wounds." —Psalm 147:3

Saying, "If you will diligently listen to the voice of the Lord your God, and do that which is right in his eyes, and give ear to his commandments and keep all his statutes, I will put none of the diseases on you that I put on the Egyptians, for I am the Lord, your healer." —Exodus 15:26

"Behold, I will bring to it health and healing, and I will heal them and reveal to them abundance of prosperity and security." —Jeremiah 33:6

"O Lord my God, I cried to you for help, and you have healed me." —Psalm 30:2

"He himself bore our sins in his body on the tree, that we might die to sin and live to righteousness. By his wounds you have been healed." —1 Peter 2:24

Zoya

Graduating from High School and Heading to College

I finally became a high school senior, and my graduation year was a momentous time. All the daydreams about leaving home and doing things that I wanted to do were very near to becoming reality, and the anticipation was thick. I was ready for the world, or so I thought. I cried after the graduation ceremony. Everything I knew was ending—class schedules, seeing the same faces, riding the school bus, etc. I did not like goodbyes. Marshall's then-husband thought it was comical that I was crying. He figured that I should be happy that I had finished school. I didn't see it that way, though. Contrary to what I thought I would feel graduation night, it did not happen that way. Things were going to change, and I didn't know anything about being an adult, having only been away from home without oversight from Mama or a sibling for school hours. All of that anticipation for all of those years caught up with me, and it didn't feel good. I had previously had wonderful thoughts about going to college, but graduating didn't feel as I thought it would at all. I had butterflies. Instead of functioning that night in a celebratory mood as my classmates were, I was a little depressed, but the anxiety was short-lived. I picked up my chin rather quickly.

I had applied to a few colleges and universities. I applied at a few Ivy League institutions as if I had been a consistent straight-A student for four years (laughable). I was a good student, but not consistently good. I was declined. I'll tell any student who wants to go to college that it's important to do well in school all the time and learn as much as you can, structured and independently . . . no distractions, no excuses. So quickly one day the SAT schedule will post, and the college application process will come. Colleges and universities will use guidelines, rules, and policies that will have nothing to do with "your desires." You had better look good on paper. Mama had talked about it with me and the others of us who were going to college. Apparently, I did look good enough on paper for a few of the schools. A college acceptance letter can change your life, change the perception of yourself, and give you a sense of "I'm good enough." It's not only about low or high self-esteem; it's about receiving the green light to go further up the education ladder as our family proudly believed in doing—and the chance to live away from home. It's one step onto the safe sidewalk of independence. Education matters. Preparing for the college life matters.

Mama didn't show very much excitement when I told her about the acceptance letters. I couldn't figure it out then. After all, my whole life she preached about going to college. Conversations in Mama's house were not about *if* we were going to college but *where we were going*. There was no debate. If we didn't have college on our agenda, our thinking was out of character for Mama's plan for us, or any plan to excel in life. It was go to college or get a new address.

After getting past the short-lived anxiety, I was excited and ready to go! What teenager wouldn't be? The first letter I received was from a college in Virginia. Mama was clear that I couldn't go there. I didn't like it one bit that she wouldn't let me go. It was one of the highest-ranking HBCUs in the country. One of the staff members was well-known because of an action she took about discrimination, which later became pivotal for the Civil Rights Movement. I wanted to meet Mrs. Stokes. I wanted to shake her hand and have long conversations with her about the hard life she had decades before and her decision to stand up against racism and discrimination in the name of justice and fairness. Perhaps I should have explained to Mama why I wanted to go to that particular college. I just pouted and applied at other colleges. Looking back, I didn't have a clue that going as far as Virginia from the deeper South would have changed a lot of things. For a mother who had successfully kept me safe and out of trouble, in her mind, allowing me to go to Virginia would be equal to sending me out of the country. After all, she was a very protective mother, particularly sheltering her daughters. In her own, unstated way, she may have wanted me near her and my two younger siblings, Sophia and Jacob.

I think Mama knew deep within that I was far from ready to enter the adult world—which is exactly what happens when you leave home to go to college. But I had to go to college, had to do what Mama had preached about all my life: get an education. I should have prepared myself better, read more, gotten better grades. Heck, I should have read the Bible and prayed more while requesting guidance and wisdom, but I did not yet know to do those things. I prayed when the family prayed and attended church regularly, but I didn't have an intimate relationship with God at the time. I was not a religious person, and I wasn't what God would have helped me to become had I asked and followed His "blueprint" in the Bible. I believed in Him, I praised Him, but I did not worship Him. There is a difference. My belief is that praising is thanking God for all the things He's done and trusting Him for what He will be doing; worshipping means serving Him, celebrating Him, living my life for Him. I strongly believe that. I wish I'd known that taking time for granted would cause me to miss opportunities for not working hard in school, and that the social life could wait. No one told me that college professors are not as forgiving, and do not give second and third chances as high school teachers may. I wish I had known or had paid more attention to the other students around me who were doing it right. I wish that I had been exposed to more things that could have better prepared me to be a college student.

Our very small town didn't have a college, but several were within a radius of two hours or less. Thankfully, my second acceptance letter came from a university that Mama approved because of its reputation and distance. It didn't have an available dormitory room at the time, so

I was on the waiting list, which meant I had to commute. I chose to attend a branch location of the same university that didn't have dormitories at all, but the commute was better, and more importantly, that campus was much smaller. Mama thought that I could adapt better for those reasons, and she was right. I did very well academically my freshman year, but life became really interesting when I transferred to the main branch when a dorm room finally became available. Oh boy, did it ever!

Yes, Mama protected us and taught us many life lessons, but by limiting our experience with other boys and girls, especially during high school years, we left home somewhat unprepared and so vulnerable. Not a good combination. In my experience, better decisions are made when you socialize with different types of people, different ethnicities, different cultures, and different beliefs. The world has no one model of anything. The world is *colorful* in more ways than one.

BE CAREFUL WHAT YOU ASK FOR

"Be careful of what you ask for." I know all too well what that means. I was excited about moving onto a college campus in a city that was more exciting than mine. As soon as I received word that a room was available on campus, I packed right away. I was excited about finally getting independence and freedom *to be me*. Mama was working when I left home, and I moved on campus without help. She didn't appear as enthusiastic as I was . . . no speech about what to do and what not to do, no "I'll see you as soon as I can." Nada. I think when she realized I was leaving, she knew things would change at home, and I'm not so sure what that even meant for her. The nest was getting closer and closer to becoming empty. I was a child who caused very little concern for her. I may have been defiant once or twice a year during high school, but I was not a troublemaker, and I did my part as a member of the family. I'm told that when I was between three and five, Dad had taken me and a few of my siblings to the store for ice cream, and my siblings were being a little rowdy, as young children can be. Dad told Mama that he would take me anywhere because I was quiet and I listened.

I was basically a quiet person for a long time, until I learned that "quiet" causes people to assume you don't have an opinion. Sometimes they discount you, don't make you relevant, and don't engage with you. There are times when a person's voice should be heard, through their writing, through discussion, or through someone else's voice. How will people truly know who you are? Speak. Write. Share experiences. Share knowledge.

Moving onto Campus

While moving into the dorm, I saw a young man was sitting at the lobby desk. Walter, the dormitory employee, was one of the hall advisors. I stopped to sign in and to get the key to my room. Walter asked, "Are you moving in today?"

I responded, "Yes." I remember thinking that he was so tall and handsome. He looked strong like an athlete. I was assigned a room on the second floor. He was not very talkative, and I didn't realize at the time that he was also a work-study student there. After I signed for my room key, he came from behind the desk to escort me to my room. I had a heavy suitcase (this was before luggage on wheels). Walter didn't offer to help me. I found that to be so unlike a gentleman. I don't recall our "small talk."

I couldn't wait to get to my room and start enjoying my semi-private space. In my mind, it would be like apartment living. Wow, what a small space; it was ridiculously small. My bedroom at home was larger, and my bed was larger, but my dorm bed was a twin size. The mattress was so thin and uncomfortable. My roommate was not there while I was moving in. Walter left after doing his hall advisor duties, telling me what I needed to know and giving me a list of phone numbers that I might need.

I soon lost control of the rapid pace of my college life. I began making choices after living a sheltered life and didn't trust anyone to help me when I was at a crossroads in college. Trusting anyone was not a comfort zone for me because I was raised not to trust others. Only a few had the chance to get to know me because for a long time, I didn't allow anyone to get too close to me.

I didn't have much to unpack at my "new residence," mostly clothes and shoes. No matter what I had or didn't have, I felt good being on my own, being where I wanted to be when I wanted to be there and with whomever I wanted to be with. I was ready to make friends; friendship was something I didn't experience outside of school hours while I lived with Mama.

It was not long before my room phone rang. I hadn't yet provided my number to anyone, so I assumed the call was for my absent roommate. No, it was Walter the hall advisor calling me. He wasted no time trying to get to know the "new dorm girl" better. I suppose he was unable to ask me out in person when he was just talking me a short time before. During the phone call, he talked about showing me around the campus and the city. I thanked him, but I didn't bite. I didn't know how to respond to the offer and didn't know if I should. I was more familiar with the city than he thought. Mama took me and my siblings there to shop, get our hair styled, visit older siblings, and attend plays and such. I came to the campus with little social experience outside of my immediate family, but I was not short of having culture and class. Mama often said, "You cannot buy class." So, I was not impressed with his initial invitation, but I knew, as green as I was, that it was his flirtatious attempt to date me or perhaps fulfill some other purpose. As Walter said after many years of marriage, "It was obvious you were green. You were fresh from your mama's wings."

My roommate eventually arrived. I'm sure she had been notified that she would have a roommate moving in. Her anticipation of what type of girl I would be probably got the best of her. It's human nature to draw conclusions and entertain preconceived notions, but it can lead us so off track.

Mama had attended nursing classes at the same university where I was attending. I think now about Mama's many accomplishments—so much determination and strength, and now her tenth child was enrolled at the college where she studied. She did everything possible to excel, and often credited that characteristic to her father.

"But he gives more grace. Therefore, it says, 'God opposes the proud, but gives grace to the humble.'"
—Elijah 4:6

"Beauty alone is not impressive." *—Anonymous*

My roommate, who looked much older, was an upperclassman at the university. It caused me to wonder if this was what getting an education does to a person. I looked youthful in comparison. She was nice, but I was turned off by her lack of neatness. Her clothes were everywhere because of limited storage space. The trash container was always overflowing. I realized quickly how different people could be. I was in for a rude awakening about others' lifestyles. Mama taught me to be clean and neat, and to have pride about my surroundings. Sharing a small space with a roommate was not fun because she seemed to have no regard for me as her roommate. She was focused on graduating, I suppose, and obviously she didn't care about my judgment, often looking skeptical of me. I saw wisdom in her eyes, but I still didn't allow myself to trust her. Not trusting others, particularly strangers, was in my DNA.

One very rare occasion while we sat on our twin beds, we had a conversation about the hall advisor. Yes, Walter came up in our conversation. Of course, she was familiar with him since they lived in the same dorm, and women usually know what's in "the crop" for harvesting. I told her about his phone call. Sarcastically, she said that he was a very studious person, and no girl was able to get close to him. I didn't know much about men or dating, but Mama had equipped me with high self-esteem. I left home not knowing squat about life, but I knew that if I wanted to date the "studious person," it could happen, ignoring my roommate.

I don't remember if it was that week or the next, but I called Walter back. It's been many years since that pivotal day, but I vividly remember. He invited me to his room. I remember the exact room and floor so well. His room number has always been an easy number to remember because I spent a lot of time there. As mentioned before, I believe our mind takes a snapshot of events and details that it wishes to remember. It was a co-ed dormitory. If Mama had known I had checked co-ed on the university's housing application, she would have intercepted. However, I didn't select co-ed to have access to a pool of males, but I wanted to be a part of something different and experience life however the world presented it. Diversity for me in my house meant girls and boys as sisters and brothers, not strange men and women in a dormitory.

I was petite with long, thick hair. I was accustomed to receiving compliments since I was a small child. I shouldn't have stayed in Walter's room as much as I did. One of the advantages of his being a hall advisor was having a larger room than other students. He cooked often and invited me to eat with him. I should have been studying instead of socializing. My behavior in those days was far from what Mama had taught me, and I was experiencing social freedom—but freedom ain't free.

When I arrived at Walter's room, I nervously knocked on his door. I was as green as a grasshopper, but I was feeling more like a grown woman, knocking at a man's door with no curfew to follow. I was living on my own. Huh! I would later find out that being under Mama's wing was the most secure place in the world for me. Walter opened the door, and I'm certain he witnessed an expression of flattery on my face. He seemed satisfied with himself that the "new, short, cute girl" was in his room and he had a shot at "something." We sat at his table. I don't recall if we ate anything but surely the man gave me a glass of Kool-Aid. I remember he made a lot of Kool-Aid during those years. We played a few card games of Spades. I learned to play the game with my siblings and was happy to show him I knew how to play. As a child, my family and I didn't do much outside home in the way of entertainment, so we played many, different games. Our family loved watching sports on television and playing several different sports as a family.

After spending hours in his room, I decided that it was time for me to go back to my room. As I walked to the door, he asked if he could kiss me. When I said, "Yes," he wanted to do more. I liked him. He was nice, but I needed to go to my room. Admittedly, I was afraid—and Mama was in that room with us (not really, but in my trained mind, she was).

We kept seeing one another, but mainly in his room—he didn't have a roommate. I started going there as a virgin, but several visits later, I didn't leave as one. I started staying overnight, which was against the dormitory rule for hall advisors at the university. Whenever someone knocked at his door, I'd hide in his bathroom.

Walter was very studious and was committed to getting his undergraduate degree. Other students would often seek his counsel for their course study. He had an analytical mind. I, on the other hand, was so fascinated with being able to live freely. I didn't concentrate on classes as I should have during my sophomore year. I skipped them sometimes. I did myself a disservice by not working hard in college during my sophomore year. I socialized and went out with friends, friends I don't call friends now. My priorities were definitely off the mark. If I only knew God then the way I know Him now. I'm confident I would have been a better student, even though I was living on my own. My freshman year was great. I commuted, and I guess for me, being at home with house rules and a "monitoring Mama" made the difference. However, I have not yet found a clock that ticks in reverse.

I learned my lesson, however, in no time. I soon soared like an eagle. It's not unheard of for anyone, including me, to make mistakes—not learning from them is what would be a waste of the error.

"If we claim to be without sin, we deceive ourselves and the truth is not is us." —1 John 1:9

THE REPERCUSSIONS OF DISOBEDIENCE

Walter graduated a year or so later. I was placed on suspension by the university. You cannot continue to make low grades and stay in school. I went to summer school in an attempt to improve my GPA. I did well in the summer classes, but two passed courses were not enough for the university's strict policies and GPA requirement. Mama, of course, was disgusted and disappointed, but as she had when I lived at home, she expressed her feelings to my siblings more than me. It was a normal state of affairs during my childhood. Judgment of others went on regularly.

If only Mama wasn't so strict with me, perhaps I would have continued commuting at the branch location and maintained the high GPA. If I'd had exposure to "real life," I would not have been fascinated with being away from home, but Mama was doing what she thought I needed at that time. Everything happens for a reason, and the reason will always be revealed, eventually. After becoming a "mature woman," which in my view is different from being a grown woman, I gained an appreciation over time for the hard work Mama put into raising me. She was the heroine that every young girl should have in her life.

I kept dating Walter and soon told him that I was moving in with my sister and her family in another city and would be going to school there. My sister lived about three hours away. I was too "green" to fathom how I would maintain a relationship with Walter. Walter and I talked on the phone, and he visited me at least once at my sister's house. She wouldn't allow him to stay at her house, and I didn't expect it. When he visited me, he checked into a hotel, but of course I could not be there with him because we were taught that a man and woman do not share a hotel room unless they are wedded, even though I broke the "no sex before marriage" rule during my sophomore year in college. I, unlike the majority of my peers, had been a virgin before then.

My sister recommended a nice hotel where Walter stayed. He appeared nervous most of the time while he visited me at her house. I suppose my sister gazing at him like he was a "husband-catch" for me made him nervous. He wasn't ready for marriage. I wasn't either. I was not even ready for a committed relationship. I was fascinated with a "dream"—dream to simply be happy. I was unaware of how "happiness" truly works, that it's not a process of osmosis. It takes planning and a lot of work and commitment.

When Walter returned to his home, I wanted to go with him after one of his visits because life for me wasn't stacking up. I wasn't a planner during those days. I knew what I wanted to do but did not know how to get it done. I didn't possess the skill of planning. At nineteen, I was a mess. I wasn't accustomed to being independent. Many teenagers even today do not have those skills. I didn't live that kind of life at home with Mama and my sisters and brothers. Cleaning the house, doing homework on time, and preparing for tests while living with your parent are not even close to being enough of what you need to know to be ready to live a responsible, independent life. I lived like a "little girl," even through high school. I wasn't guided as I wish I had been in preparation for being on my own. That takes a concentrated effort while raising a child. I was horribly sheltered. Although not productive for me, I understand now why it was that way and how things easily got out of hand. As many say once they become adults, *I wish I knew then what I know now.* I wish I had had a relative or friend or even a stranger to tell me that trouble doesn't last always . . . as the gospel song goes. I wish someone had told me that God is our dearest friend and takes care of us, that we can be assured that everything is going to be okay, and that I should wholeheartedly give it to Him. But God had work to do with me and the people in my family, as well as the people I had not even met yet. The old adage that "knowledge is power" surely has more weight to it than I imagined during those tender years.

Speaking of raising a child, at twenty, I became pregnant. I was not saddened about being pregnant, but I was mortified about telling Mama. She had preached so often about getting an education and being married before becoming a parent. I was happy to be "with child," but I did not have a clue how my life would move forward with no job and a currently incomplete college degree. I was so afraid. This was something Mama didn't want to see happen to me or any of her daughters before she at least completed college — but the one thing that would not, could not, happen is that we bring a child into the world before getting married. In those years, it was socially unacceptable to be pregnant and not married. Wow! How drastically life has changed.

But getting married just for the purpose of having

a marital status is never good. I did so for various reasons. Other than those reasons mentioned and Mama's demand, I wanted my baby to have the "model scenario." I remember the expressions of "I'm not ready for a family" and "I have plans for my life" on Walter's face. Mama was not having it and instructed me to call Walter to pick me up. I was at Mama's when he came. I may not have had much life experience and may have acted irresponsibly, but one of the *best* decisions I've ever made was convincing Walter to pick me up and marry me so I could start a respectable life. I wanted my baby. I wanted to be married.

When Walter came to Mama's, he was not enthusiastic about what was on her mind. Mama was committed to marrying off her daughter. Walter was interviewing for a job. He was taking the right steps for his life. Looking back, he took responsible steps for his future. He tried to explain to Mama that he wanted to get a job and get stable before taking on a family, and he would come back for me, but Mama was not having it; she did not want to trust it. Her facial expression and stern voice told him he was taking me with him because we needed to start our life together. He did, but that decision along with all decisions leading up to that evening would prove pivotal to lives that I could not have imagined as a twenty-year-old. But I felt better, despite the factors surrounding the drama. I did not have to give up my child. My child would have their father and me together.

I knew that it wasn't a totally happy moment when Walter took me with him, and it was stressful for him, Mama, and me. Operating with naiveté, I thought I could be a good wife and mother. Well, one out of two proved to be true. Walter and I both had no business uniting in marriage. We did not even know ourselves; living life in a "grown-up world" was much more than we bargained for. We made one of the biggest mistakes of our lives when we married before we were ready for *the married life*. However, having my baby girl was a champion move, and one I've never regretted.

———————————

"It's okay to fall. It's okay to ask for help; it's okay to be vulnerable. It's okay to get up and make no apologies to anyone for falling, even if you fell down dozens of times, but when you rise, do not look for applause; do not look for a parade. Be better for you. Humility is important. Once you go through humility and remorse and yes, even learn about self-love, you will treat yourself better, and when you love yourself as GOD created you to, you will love those around you correctly. You cannot care for others without regard for caring for yourself (the right way, the healthy way)." —Anonymous

———————————

LIFE INTERRUPTED

Walter looked at his plans as interrupted, but sustainable. He was baffled by what was happening. I suppose he felt his life was spinning out of control. Again, he had a plan for his future that didn't include a wife and a child, at least not that soon. After we went to the courthouse to get married, it was not long before he grew cold toward me. He started a great career and I worked. We led a life that afforded us the chance to buy nice houses and cars, and even had a budget to travel over time. However, we both behaved immaturely as a wife and husband. Material things really do not make a person happy, at least not a happiness that lasts forever. When night falls, you want to be held, talked to *gently*, with *inclusion*, and *lovingly*, and have conversations about the future.

To be honest, we weren't friends first: Mistake #1. We became lovers after dating such a very short while, and didn't use the formula for building a meaningful, healthy relationship. He had his faults and I had mine. We were much too young to build a life as husband and wife; we barely knew ourselves as individuals. The one thing Walter had that I did not was the privilege of being raised by both parents; he had a father in the home his entire life. That can make a difference, *if* the father is treating his family well and directing his children as God teaches us. I didn't have my father in my life since he died when I was about five, but I stand by the embarrassing belief that my life would have been much worse if I had him in it. Who would prefer an alcoholic, abusive father? I'm grateful that God did not prevent some things from happening, even the painful ones.

Suffering strengthens if kept in the right perspective. In later years, life became better and better, yet it took time. God worked on us, and He kept on working. We needed God, and He never left us.

"Train up a child in the way he should go: and when he is old, he will not depart from it."—Proverbs 22:6

"The LORD trieth the righteous: but the wicked and him that loveth violence his soul hateth."—Psalms 11:5

"You cannot climb to the top of a mountain if the sides are smooth."—Anonymous

---

STARTING A FAMILY

Walter and I had a daughter, Paige. We were great parents, considering we were young and things didn't start out under the best of circumstances. We doted on her and were supported by our families with clothes, books, and advice. I was a stay-at-home mom for the first three years of her life. I did not want anyone else caring for her. Walter, Paige, and I lived too far from family to ask them to help care for her if I had worked. I was determined to keep her at home (no daycare nor babysitter) until she could talk well enough for me and her dad to understand her words.

I read so many magazines and books about how to care for her in every aspect. I watched parenting shows on TV, which was such a big help for me. Walter and I read to her and taught her to read to us before she was old enough to attend kindergarten. Mama had often told me what to do concerning getting Paige prepared for school and what to do when she became ill with colds and fever. Walter and I were very fortunate with having so many experienced parents as family members. That was a blessing.

We visited vacation spots in the Virgin Islands, Florida, Georgia, New York, DC, New Jersey, Tennessee, North Carolina, and the list got longer over the years. We also took her to church and read a children's Bible to her until she could read it on her own. No matter where we relocated to, we found a church to go to. We wanted Paige to know the importance of attending church and worshipping. She performed well in school, even though she had to change schools because of our job assignments, making us proud each year. Walter wanted me to find a job when I was well enough to work after Paige was born. I insisted on staying home until our daughter reached the age of three. I was adamant about her not being cared for by anyone else until she could communicate well about her day. We lived in a few different states due to company relocations, but going to a new school did not cause a hiccup for Paige. She was a determined and focused student.

Our daughter was a priority. Later we had a son, Shane, the brother Paige had been waiting for. She had asked her dad and me for a brother or a pet. She got the better of the options. Shane made her life even more "special." She cared for him so lovingly and protectively without wavering. Our son was a joy from the time it was confirmed that I was pregnant with him. I knew he would be a boy. Some things a woman just knows. I could not wait to meet my son. Paige helped to name her brother. She was a viable part of Shane's life from the very beginning. I've never heard of a child waiting for a sibling's arrival and celebrating his coming into the world as Paige did. We were blessed to have children with such an unprecedented, close relationship. Although our marriage ended, we had two wonderful children. The best thing that happened in my life was having Paige and Shane.

I could say that our marriage was doomed from the beginning. Looking back, I was not a good girlfriend, and he really didn't like that his life had been interrupted with having a family earlier than he had planned. I don't think he processed that my life, too, was interrupted. Walter was not an affectionate man during those years. He sometimes was not supportive and made me feel less than a partner — not by what he said so much but what he didn't say as well as his "emotional absence." Although there were times he'd say things that stopped me in my tracks, I will never say that our marriage failed *because of him only*. Marital failure is never the fault of one party. My role was deep-rooted. I made marital mistakes, and I own up to them, but he never owned up to his, at least not to me. In his mind, the failed marriage was my fault, and I know that no failed marriage is ever one person's fault. Like a coin has two sides, so does a story. Most people feel comfortable telling about others' chapters of life events but exclude their own participation . . . their own chapters.

The tricky thing about that: *the truth surfaces sooner or later.*

Marshall

We Add to Our Family

At age twenty-six, in October the year following my college graduation, I gave birth to another daughter, Sarah. They placed her pink bassinet in the middle of the six blue bassinets. Lily and Claire, six and five years old respectively, were so excited to have a little sister.

Not long after Sarah was born, we received orders to a base in the Midwest. I hated to leave my brother and sisters again, but they were all in high school or college now, and David had already received his commission as a second lieutenant and was assigned out of state. We arrived at our next base and rented an apartment nearby. It was easy then as a military member to enroll the children in a new school. Roger decided to buy a house and stop paying rent, so we purchased a house near the base. Sarah was learning to walk and my youngest sister Sophia, age sixteen, came to visit for the summer. The house was new construction on a cul-de-sac. It had a fireplace, a sunken living room, three bedrooms, two bathrooms, a laundry room, a very nice kitchen, and a dining area.

It also had a large yard and a two-car garage. I thought we had arrived! The mortgage lending rates were in the double digits back then. The car Mama had given me had stopped working, and Roger actually bought a new family car. He showed up with it without any input from me. Before this purchase, he would only buy sports cars, namely the Datsun 240z or 260z — a most uncomfortable car for a child, let alone three children. Back then you did not need car seats. When we traveled to visit family back home, I would ride in the back with two of the children so they could take turns being comfortable in the front passenger seat. Roger would never allow me to drive when he was in the car.

I was a home childcare giver to help pay the bills, charging $75 a week per child. I needed to send money to Mama to help her pay for my brother and sisters' clothes and shoes, books, etc., and help with anything else she or they needed. Finally, I got a job at the base working part-time. My hours were 5:00 p.m.–9:00 p.m. so we didn't need to pay for childcare. It so happened that Roger and I worked in the same building, so I would drive to the building and wait for him to come out and transfer the girls from my car to his. I worked this job for 364 days. I planned to get pregnant with a boy in September of 1983, so that my son would be born in my birth month. I followed a recipe to increase the odds of having a boy.

Our son, Cuyler, was born the day before Father's Day the following year. Roger was told by the nurse that he had a son, but he didn't believe her and wanted to see for himself if it really was a boy. He had been told before that he had a son when one of the girls was born.

So he saw our son's private parts with his own eyes and thanked God and promised Him that day that he would stop drinking. Apparently, Roger had made a deal with the Lord that if He gave him a son, he would give up drinking alcohol, and, as far as I knew, he never drank again. After ten years of hoping and praying that Roger would stop drinking, it seems I got my wish. I often wondered why he drank anyway. Unlike Daddy, who became mean and abusive when he drank, Roger didn't appear to change at all.

Roger's longest assignment had never been longer than two years, and this one was no exception. He received orders to another state in the Midwest, which meant we had to hurriedly try to sell the house with the astronomical interest rate. Since it wasn't selling fast enough, Roger decided to carry the loan for the only interested buyers, another military family. We closed quickly and said our goodbyes to the family, with whom we had grown extremely close. Little did I know during our many dinners, cookouts, and card games that Roger had known the couple since his first officer's training assignment way back in October of 1975. The wife, Cindy, and I did everything together, and our children were always with us. Cindy and I even worked part-time at the same unit on base, and we took courses at the same college but on different days of the week so that we could keep each other's children when we had our classes. I finished my real estate agent licensing course and Cindy graduated with a Bachelor's degree. Since she received little support from her husband to achieve her goal of a college degree, I helped her in every way I could to be successful in that endeav-

or, which she achieved. She was the first in her family to graduate from college.

We moved with our three daughters and son to our next assignment. Since our marriage in June of 1975, Roger had been assigned to five different bases in fewer than ten years. Emma called my children and me gypsies because we were always moving, never taking root anywhere. Oddly, she never included Roger in that gypsy status, even though we were moving because of his work. I had also completed the goal I'd had since I was twelve years old: having four children.

Throughout our many assignments, I would send for my sisters over holidays and summers. Usually, Mama would let only Sophia come because Emma had dibs on Goya to keep her children during those times. Roger knew and seemed to appreciate that we would have my sisters with us whenever Mama would allow them to come. At one time or another, Charlotte, Jacob, and Sophia lived with us and went to school wherever we lived. When we were stationed close to our hometown, Goya came to visit almost every weekend after she finished her classes at college. Mama, Emma, and her family, as well as Charlotte, Goya, Jacob, and Sophia, even visited for several days at our first assignment.

Looking back, I think Mama sensed that all was not well with child #7 (the top of the bottom six of her children) and insisted on driving out to see for herself. I could not believe that all of them came in one car. Mama said she would make the drive herself, so Emma's husband insisted on coming because he didn't want Mama traveling that distance by herself with four children in tow. I was disappointed that their visit was so short, and I wanted so badly to go back with them. I cried and cried for days after they left. I had learned from my sisters that their letters to me had been all lies. Emma had told them for months that they had better not burden me with their little problems.

Now our family of six moved to a much larger base where Roger was a squadron commander. I was a stay-at-home mom again at this new assignment. We lived in substandard base housing, which meant that Roger was able to keep part of his housing allowance. The girls were enrolled in school and were bussed off-base to the closest elementary school. I baked bread and made their lunches, each made to order based on their condiment preferences, with pickles, drink, and fruit of their choosing. At this point, Cuyler would wait at the screen door every school day, always sensing that his sisters would be arriving soon. I always had their snacks ready. I thought I was Betty Crocker Suzy Homemaker.

When I questioned Roger about him being unfaithful, I was still so naïve that I believed every word out of his lying mouth. Years later, a woman I considered my "friend" told me that Roger had been cheating on me since right after the birth of our first child.

Two years later, after Roger received an assignment to Bristol, I was confronted once again with the irrefutable proof of his infidelity. Because I did not want to move the children to the big city which we had heard nothing good about, we decided that Roger would move unaccompanied for his assignment, and the children and I would stay at Mama's for the duration of this two-year tour. I was so excited that I would be back at Mama's to help in any way I could, even though Charlotte and David had long since left home. Goya, too, had married and moved away. Jacob and Sophia were away at college. Mama initially agreed that we could live with her, but after she had apparently consulted with Emma, she put the kibosh on that plan. Even though our movers were splitting our household goods based on the original plan and Roger had already secured a one-year lease on a one-bedroom apartment near his work, he had to have our things re-routed to storage in the Bristol area.

Roger took a flight down so he could drive us all back in my old Ford car. Even though my family thought it was a disgrace that Roger let us drive around in that raggedy car, I liked it, and it suited my purposes because we could all fit in it. It was white with a brown interior, and it even had a fold-down seat in the wagon part which Cuyler and Sarah loved to sit in because it faced backwards. Roger had not changed in his desire to always have a sports car—another Z, this time a 260z. Despite the fact that he had sired four children, he never wanted it to look like he was a family man.

Once Roger collected us from Mama's, we began the drive to Bristol. During the drive, he planned how we would all be able to live in his one-bedroom apartment until base housing came through without management finding out that we were a family of six. Roger's plan was that we could never be seen as a family of six, and so we never left the apartment as a group. He would always leave the apartment with Lily and Sarah, and I would leave with Claire and Cuyler. We never left or returned through the front entrance where we might be seen and asked questions. Inside the apartment, we tried to keep the children quiet so that neighbors wouldn't know that so many people were in the apartment.

Roger also told me that I would have to find a job once we were assigned base housing because the children would have to go to private school once we moved. No schools near the base were considered good or safe enough for our children. Roger and I argued constantly about his desire to put me out to work and my desire to be a stay-at-home mom. I'll never forget our final argument on the subject when he said to me, "You'll never find a job anyway. Who would hire you even with a college degree?" I was so hurt but this time, I remembered my college professor's words: "He is not hurting you. *You are allowing him to hurt you.*" I used Mama's words and told Roger, "You will regret the day and damn the hour that you ever said that to me."

It was as if he were attacking Mama's dream for all of her children. She wanted us all to graduate from a four-year college.

The following morning, I loaded my four children into the car we called "Old Betsy" and headed to the base where we would be living in a few weeks' time. There was so much traffic! I was scared to death but got on the beltway; not having Google Maps or WAZE then, I tried to use a paper map and my memory of when Roger had shown us the base where we would be living to try to find my way back there. I was completely lost, going around in circles. I finally found my way back to the apartment parking lot. Still in the car, crying and praying for God's help, I asked Him to direct my path to the base so that I could apply for a job. This time, He led me straight to the base's personnel office without error or incident. Wearing what I called my housewife uniform, a sweatshirt and matching sweatpants, I took my four kids and entered the scary old brick building located right inside the security gates. I must have looked so sad and pitiful. The children were cooperating and sat quietly while I filled out the civilian personnel application for employment form. I didn't know at the time that I would complete many such forms before my career ended.

After completing the application, I corralled my kids and headed toward the exit. One of the personnel management specialists called me back and said, "There's an opening as an administrative assistant across the street at Security Police. Would you like to go for an

interview now?"

I looked down at my housewife uniform and over at my brood of children and replied, "Yes. Thank you." I knew she felt sorry for me and was trying to help me out. She called ahead to tell them that I would be right over for an interview.

My kids and I walked across the street to the Security Police Squadron; once there, I was directed to the basement, where I was greeted by Fiona, the woman who would be my supervisor. We hit it off right from the start, and she asked when I would be able to start. Before considering all the roadblocks, such as transportation, gas, and childcare, I replied, "As soon as possible." We walked across the street, got back in the car, and drove back to the apartment, again without incident—until we tried to go in through the back door of the apartment building. It was locked! We had no choice but to go through the front of the building. The lobby was completely empty, so we scurried to the nearest elevator and up to the seventh floor, letting out a sigh of relief when we made it to the apartment without seeing another soul. Thank you again, God.

_____

"Build up, build up, prepare the road! Remove the obstacles out of the way of my people." —Isaiah 57-14

_____

That evening, after Roger got home from work, the telephone rang. It was the personnel office, offering me the job at Security Police. I was so scared, but I refused to let Roger see it. I calmly accepted the offer and matter-of-factly said to him, "I start a week from Monday." I also reiterated to him that he would regret the day and damn the hour that he ever challenged me or tried to belittle me.

My start date would allow me to find childcare for Cuyler on base. We had already enrolled the girls in a really good private school in Berlin, and the base would bus them there once we moved. Thank God, our name came up to the top on the military base family housing list because we had so many children. Imagine that—having four children was finally a plus. Roger had to break the apartment lease, but he reconciled losing the deposit with the fact that he would save by living in base housing.

When I received my first biweekly paycheck, Roger informed me that it was my responsibility to pay for Cuyler and Sarah's childcare. Sarah was in kindergarten, so the bus would pick her up from the private school at midday and take her to the base childcare facility where her brother was being cared for. After the first day there, when I found my son still crying as I picked him up, I could stand it no longer and found a woman on base who was a former school teacher and a licensed child caregiver. She already had five children of her own but was allowed to keep up to three more. I told her I would pay her extra to keep Cuyler all day and Sarah for half days. She accepted and actually fell in love with Cuyler. By the time I finished paying her for the care of my children, I was left with $40 dollars every two weeks. I suppose this was another way for Roger to exhibit control.

I worked for Fiona at Security Police for four and a half months before being offered a higher grade at another headquarters. During that time, Fiona had put me in for several monetary awards that I received. She helped me in every way she could and wrote reference letters that would ensure me success in being considered for my next grade level. Although I hated leaving Fiona, I needed to make more money, so I accepted a job that would take me to the next level. I had another really wonderful female supervisor at my next job. She too ensured I received every award she could put me in for. After two years within that directorate, I applied for and was selected for a higher GS position at another government office.

By now, I was at a point where I felt valued by everyone in my work life—but not by my husband, the person who should have been lifting me up was trying to put me down every chance he got. His attempts to degrade and belittle me, however, had the opposite effect. The very accomplished, very tall, very handsome and very attentive new man at work, my work husband, thought I was wonderful, beautiful, and smart, and he made me feel appreciated every day. He became my confidante in all matters and remains so. Every Friday, the office had drinks in the workplace. This was back when that sort of thing was allowed or at least not frowned upon. And most Friday nights, the staff would leave work and head to the trendiest night spot in the area. This time marked the best time of my adult life up until that point. I was happy at work, but married life became a chore. We considered divorce several times but stayed married for the sake of the children. I do not recommend this for anyone.

After several promotions and the substantial increase in his housing allowance, Roger decided to move us off base, rent a house, and pocket the extra money. Claire and Lily were enrolled in public middle and high schools. Cuyler was in first grade, and Sarah was in the third grade in the elementary school right across the street from the house. We stayed in the suburbs for exactly one school year and then Roger decided that it was not a good fit for the children. So we moved back on base that summer, right next door to the house we had moved from just a year before.

Lily and Claire tested into the best public charter high school, and Sarah and Cuyler were enrolled in the best public elementary schools in the more affluent area of the city. The Department of Defense bussed them all to these schools, so we felt that the children were quite safe even in this city of very high crime rates. The children were always well liked and participated in sports both on base and in school. During Cuyler's third grade year, Roger received orders for an unaccompanied assignment. This would also be Lily's last year of high school and Sarah's last year of middle school. Over my objections, Roger decided to return to the States halfway through his assignment and take Cuyler back with him for the remaining six months of the tour. This was around Christmas time, and so I packed up Cuyler's things and he went off to spend the last half of his third-grade year with his dad. I spent those six months preparing Lily for college. We applied to about thirteen colleges and universities and she was accepted to all but two of them.

When Roger and Cuyler returned that summer, the Christmas tree was still as it was when my son left. I had decided to keep it up until he safely returned home. Because of his learning disability, Cuyler would require a lot of help in school when he returned. Sarah, we decided, should attend private school. Because we would be paying college tuition that year and the following year and helping nieces who were also in college or starting at the same time, with the help of a very well-connected uncle, Sarah's private school tuition was paid in full by a wealthy benefactor. After ninth grade, Sarah tested and was accepted at the same public charter high school that her sisters had attended. Both her sisters were valedictorians and had received multiple grants and scholarships.

Claire had received the most scholarship money ever received at the time. The summer after her graduation, she also received monetary gifts for her education from constituents of a politician who were friends of that same very well-connected uncle.

Saying Goodbye to the "Love of Your Life"

I met the love of my life during this assignment . . . but it could not be. I could not leave my children. Why is it that you meet the love of your life *after* you get married? We met over the telephone while he was on assignment to Africa. Having accepted a position in Australia, he asked me to accompany him there, but I could not leave my children. Even now, after all these intervening years, I still miss him. I was my absolute best with him. This relationship did not go unnoticed by Roger, yet he did nothing to stop it—why would he? He was in a relationship with his secretary, who lived on the same street. She was everything I was not. She dressed provocatively and was draped over a man every chance she got. Some men must like this kind of pretentious, doting behavior. That was not me—at least not with a man who showed me no love or respect.

On the day I had to say goodbye to the love of my life, the sun was shining brightly as I dropped him at the airport. However, I was crying so hard that I thought it was raining, so I turned on the wipers. Fellow drivers must have thought I was crazy. I know it to be true that the heart hurts even if you're not having angina or a heart attack. Heartache is actually a physical pain. Something else I know to be true in love: The mind forgets . . . but the heart remembers.

I now know why Mama cried because it's why I've cried . . .

- Because I was an abused daughter; because I was an abused sister; because I was an abused niece; because I was an abused student; because I was an abused wife; because I was an abused friend; because I was an abused employee.

- And many, many times over, I cried because I was happy, for myself and for many others.

- Like Mama, I cried because I was touched or saddened, or maybe a family member achieved something no one thought we would.

- Many times as a mother or sibling I was overwhelmed, my heart so full of love and pride and gratefulness that it poured from my eyes.

I now know why Mama cried.

Zoya

Unhappy Marriage

I certainly realized that if I could be emotionally unhappy in a marriage that had no physical abuse, then
Mama must have been *totally miserable in hers*. She
experienced all types of abuse with Dad. I can say with
empathy that I know why Mama cried. After being married for fourteen years, Walter and I divorced. Divorce
is never an easy process, especially when children are
involved. Walter and I kept our children in mind with
every step, even post-divorce. We never wanted them to
hurt because of the bad decisions their parents had made.
It was tough for them at times, not having both parents
in the house together, but not nearly as tough as it could
have been if we were not constantly keeping our children
as our first and main priority.

I struggled financially for many years post-divorce
from Walter. Statistics show that women don't do as well
as men do after a divorce. It helped to have child support, but taking care of children is not an easy task. In
my view, then and now, children must be well cared for
in every way, and sacrifices must be made for them. My
children never wanted for anything. They lived a privileged life and were shown love and support in a way that
unfortunately some children don't experience.

I knew despite how well they were cared for, they

didn't want their parents to be separated. I never followed the divorce decree where it outlined a schedule that stated when Walter could have them in his care. Whenever he wanted to visit them or needed me to take them to him—like times it meant me going with them on a plane because of their age—that's what I did without a second thought. I was never petty in that way. I sent information to him about everything that was going on in their lives, including report cards, their scheduled school events, pictures of their events, birthday celebration plans, etc. Walter was very involved; he was a very active father, and I did not want to discourage or hamper the relationship with our kids in any way. It takes a concerted, committed effort to raise healthy children when their parents have divorced. I made sure they kept a close relationship with their father, never wanting them to feel any pain about having divorced parents. I certainly was never going to have them feeling that their parents' separation was their fault. My children were and have been my life.

God surely knows all of it. Divorce isn't easy on a family, and the older of my two felt the effects more than the younger one because of age difference. My son was only a toddler at the time. He was certainly happy to be wherever his sister was because they were very close then as they are now. I taught them to love and protect one another, and to let no one come between them. They were blessed children in so many ways because of their dad, many family members, and me, and certainly because of God's guidance.

Married and Divorced — Again

I married again, but I shouldn't have. I jumped into another relationship too fast. My second husband, Antonio, and I didn't know each other long enough. We knew that we were comfortable around one another and felt happy. He was a kind man. He was quite a bit older than I was. Antonio was attentive, and he adored me. Sometimes, an older man treats a woman differently, more like a lady and with patience and understanding. This, of course, isn't always the case, but it was for me as well as many women I've talked to over the years. He knew that my children meant the world to me and that they came first. Children must feel important, loved, supported, and never second to anyone, and mine had that with a triple dose.

Antonio had children who were grown. He didn't have a close relationship with any of them, so after we married, I attempted to mend the fences between them, but with no success. The scars were too deep, for whatever reasons. He soon became ill and was in pain daily, all day long for years, though it was bearable enough to do things for himself. Antonio eventually became depressed, and before long, he said he thought it was best for us to go our separate ways. Deep in my heart, I believe he felt that he (as an ill man) was a burden to a woman with young children. He wanted me to continue concentrating on them. Antonio could see that I was not going to compromise my relationship with my children and their dad was never to be left out their life in no degree.

Antonio's life had been lived much differently than mine. He had not been a good parent to his biological children when they were younger. Many of his past years were troubled. I didn't find out until later about the many events in his younger years and his time as an army veteran. He was kind and as fatherly as he could be to Paige and Shane, while Walter remained very active in their lives. During my marriage to Antonio, I still made sure that they visited their dad as often as possible and talked on the phone with him anytime they wanted to.

I believe Antonio secretly envied how Walter and I parented. His outlook on life and his past were invariably different. Sometimes, it's not until you are deeply in something that a bright light shines on the truth, and you realize it was a mistake. We loved one another, *but love just wasn't enough*. Our mindset about how life should be lived was not a match. Antonio wanted me to be with him as much as possible. However, my children were still young at the time (elementary and high school). I spent time catering to their needs as students and living life as healthily as possible, and I wanted them to maintain the very close relationship they had with their father and their father's family. Antonio and I didn't compare notes before the "I do." How reckless, how irresponsible, how disconnected to reality we were. The marriage was regrettably short-lived. Antonio and I sold the house — the very nice house he only agreed to buy to please my children and me, because he knew we were accustomed to having a nice home in a nice neighborhood in a highly-rated school district. Antonio did many things for us, not necessarily because he had to have it that way for himself.

We had accumulated very few assets as husband and wife, so deciding on who would get anything we owned was not a problem. It was an amicable divorce. For a time, I stayed in touch with his sister to get updates about him. Thankfully, she appreciated my efforts and shared details about his health. I was very appreciative and was comforted that he had a caring sister who stuck by him until his death.

Didn't Let Grass Grow Under My Feet

Life for my children and me kept moving along. Although I felt the disappointment of another failed marriage, I was not inclined to feel sorry for myself. I had children to continue raising and supporting, and it was my responsibility to propel them to the next level and the next. I had to be careful with their emotions and wellbeing as well—after all, they were experiencing another divorce too.

My daughter was getting closer to graduating from high school and had applied to several colleges, including a few Ivy League schools. My son was continuing on in elementary school. I signed him up to play for youth football and baseball leagues. Time kept on passing, and soon, it was senior prom night for Paige. I bought Paige a beautiful gold gown. She went to the hair salon for a stylish up-do and got a fresh manicure and pedicure. It was important that my daughter had the entire prom experience. She deserved it. Her date was a handsome fella who played basketball at her high school, and he arrived in a limo. Paige had a wonderful prom experience, and Shane took delight in watching every moment.

My daughter was soon leaving the nest. Paige had been a very good and well-rounded student. Her reputation in all the schools she had attended was stellar. She was active in extracurricular activities and worked an internship during high school. Initiating a relationship with the lead partner of a law firm, she interned there until she graduated from high school. Paige had always displayed a hunger to succeed. She mentored her brother and peers to do the same. Several colleges accepted her application, including a few of the Ivy League institutions.

Sadly, I had to advise her of the financial aspect. Acceptance letters are great to read, but if the school doesn't pay the bill to attend, particularly if it's out of state, attending is not feasible. College tuition is notoriously expensive. Other great schools wanted her as well, so she narrowed it down. When she made her final decision to attend a college twelve hours away from home, I was okay with that because I had made up my mind to relocate to the same city. Oh yes. Paige was only sixteen as an early high school graduate, and I had no intention of letting her be so far away from me; besides, her brother would have missed her terribly. A plus was that I would be able to see Mama more regularly since the college was near the area where she lived. In my estimation, it was a win-win decision. I have no regrets about moving to be close to my daughter and to keep my children near one another. They had a bond that I was determined to keep glued together. I wanted them to have with one another what I had with a few of my twelve siblings, who truly knew how important it is to love and support family . . . to support my children and me during challenging times. I've learned that people cannot give what they have not been given unless they step out of *self* and love as God's word teaches us.

"*. . . do not merely look out for your own personal interests, but also for the interests of others. Have this attitude in yourselves which was also in Christ Jesus, who, although He existed in the form of God, did not regard equality with God a thing to be grasped, but emptied Himself, taking the form of a bond-servant, and being made in the likeness of men. Being found in appearance as a man, He humbled Himself by becoming obedient to the point of death, even death on a cross.*" —*Philippians 2:4-8*

WE'RE MOVING! NEW LIFE, NEW ADDRESS

Paige made her college choice, and we were moving. Shane was excited to be going with his sister. I was divorced for the second time, and once again, it was just the three of us. I looked forward to the move. My daughter would have her brother and me at her fingertips rather than twelve hours away. I was satisfied. Our friends could not believe that my son and I were going to relocate where my daughter was going to college. I had found our new home and told my family about our move. It was not even a difficult decision for me. Wherever my daughter was going to college, that's where we were going. I needed to be near her. We had stuck together through everything, her dad was living far away at the time, and she *was* going to have one of her parents nearby. I told her dad the plan from the beginning, and he was on board with it. He knew that he could depend on me to support our daughter, and he would be doing his part as well.

My children are not only my heart, but also my heartbeat. I haven't always made the best decisions, but I have always thought of raising productive, loving, caring Christians as one of my purposes in life. As grown people, now they are all that and more. Many parents have stories of disappointments. I do not. Sure, my children made minor mistakes that come with being children and learning, but nothing to cause major concerns, not even close.

So, the moving company packed us up, and we loaded our van with all our personal items to hold us until the truck arrived at our new home; then we were headed southeast, back to my home state. My children and I drove twelve hours, and it felt good. I was their mama and we were on our journey together.

I found a job very soon after moving to the city where my daughter was going to college, but after a few years, I eventually left that first job. The work environment and circumstances were not "comfortable." I wished so many times I had completed my college degree years before. I couldn't even apply for many lucrative jobs because I lacked an undergraduate degree. I could out-skill and out-work the best of them, but so many employers didn't care. I didn't have that required "piece of paper" that

Mama often described as the dealbreaker if you didn't have it. Mama was so right.

After a short while, I found another job. I had to settle for something I really didn't want to do, but I needed to work. Many positions became available at the company and I couldn't apply. Managers would ask me to apply for them and I embarrassingly told them I didn't have a degree. They were surprised because I wrote well, spoke well, and worked like a professional. I felt like kicking myself on the butt for the mistakes I made during my college years, but then, who doesn't make mistakes? You cannot dwell on them; you have to forge forward to being better.

―――――――――

"When you mess up, it bothers you more than when someone else messes up things for you. Mistakes can hurt and majorly affect your road to success, and if you don't see that the mistake is only a missing step on the ladder and that you just have to stretch higher to the next step, you won't get back on track." —Goya

"I will rather boast about my weaknesses, so that the power of Christ may dwell in me." —2 Cor. 12:9

―――――――――

MAMA WAS LIVING A BETTER LIFE

Mama was living alone in the same small town, but she was dating again. Mama had known Michael for many years. They had met at the age of fourteen and liked one another; they lost touch but rediscovered one another many years later. He was from a small town near Wesville. He was very tall and slender, was respected as the head basketball coach, and had a decent reputation. Mama liked him a lot.

Michael and Mama had been dating for quite a while by the time I had moved back near her home to live. She and I had talked about Michael during our phone calls, and my siblings and I often teased her about him. I was back home but nonetheless, if I wanted to visit her, I needed to check with her for availability because she and Michael traveled and hung out often. Mama had it going on! Raising twelve children and getting through a difficult life were not going to put her social/romantic life on pause.

My siblings and I were pleased about her relationship with Michael. He was a respected, retired coach, and Mama loved sports. They went to high school games often. Mama had been through so much with Dad and her family that she deserved a loving relationship without twisted bouts of abuse. All her children had long left the roost, and it was her time to live life to the fullest. Mama had earned a college degree, secured a few lucrative jobs over the years, owned her house, and was driving a snazzy car. For an abused Black mother of twelve, that deserves the highest recognition attainable.

All of us, my siblings and I, liked Michael. We were so happy that the two of them found love again. They liked traveling to the beach, attending sports events, and eating at local restaurants. Mama was experiencing a relationship with a man that any woman would be attracted to. She continued being very private about a lot of her personal business, so it was not known right away that Michael had become seriously ill. I think a few of my siblings knew just because it didn't take long for news to travel in the small town where they lived. Mama ultimately confided to a few of us that Michael was ill. She was visiting him in the hospital frequently. Then, he eventually succumbed to his illness.

Many people in town who knew him for so long were saddened. We were saddened for Mama. She had been having such good times with him. They both always seemed happy when they were together. When Michael passed away, Mama mourned but mostly privately. Mama handled most aspects of her life privately . . . even her valleys. She didn't have another companion after Michael passed. She was aging and slowing down. Several of her children checked on her and did whatever we could to keep her equipped with things she needed, and to simply show love and concern for her wellbeing.

Mama was very independent, which made it difficult to initiate too much without her knowledge and input. She did not like being asked a lot of questions, and she certainly wasn't going to volunteer much of her personal information. Being her children did not give us carte blanche. Mama operated on a "need-to-know basis" to a fault, and so do I. Mama often said, "If you tell your busi-

ness, you won't have any for yourself. People are not going to keep your business confidential. They cannot help
themselves." She was prophetically correct in so many
ways. Mama was hurt many times by people she told her
most intimate experiences to and yet they betrayed her
by telling others. Trusting others was understandably a
challenge for her.

MAMA'S SIGNS OF DECLINE

After a few years passed, I noticed Mama was becoming
forgetful. She would misplace her purse or car keys and,
frustrated, say that someone took her purse or keys from
her house. At the time, I lived only twenty-five to thirty
minutes away. When we talked on the phone, she would
not ask me to come help her find them. Mama was prideful and never liked bothering or depending on anyone.
If you told her that you could do something for her and
she liked the idea, she would allow it. I would always
volunteer to go to her house and help find whatever she
had misplaced. I didn't want to believe that anyone in
our family had stolen from her. No one had; I would find
the item each time I searched. Mama had actually hidden
her purse or keys or both in a cabinet or a drawer; in her
mind, she was securing her possessions in case someone
came to her house. I didn't want her to worry. I wanted
her to be able to go to sleep knowing all her personal be-
longings were in place. No matter when she called with
the story that someone "took" her purse or keys, I'd go to
her rescue to resolve her concern.

One night was a school night for my son, and I had

already tucked him in bed; but after another call from Mama about her missing keys, I wrapped Shane, about seven, in a blanket, put him in my car, and drove to Mama's. I knew Mama would not be at peace until she had her purse in hand; I didn't want her feeling stressed. When I got there, she looked confused. She could not understand how her purse was not where she put it. She mentioned that someone had visited her and must have taken it, and until I found her purse, I had to at least think it was possible. I searched her house and eventually looked in cabinets and drawers. I remembered the days when Grandma misplaced her things. She also would say someone stole them. I remembered she too would become infuriated as I experienced with Mama.

I would get so happy after finding Mama's purse or keys. I didn't want to go home without relieving my Mama. When she realized that her purse had been in a drawer all along, she said, "What was it doing in there? Who put it there?" I assured her that she had and had forgotten about it. Mama, as Grandma, was always guarded when she knew anyone would be visiting. I didn't think, at the time, that it was uncommon for aging people.

Mama continued misplacing her things or forgetting about something, but I loved her so much and didn't want her to worry, I never made any condescending, reckless comments to her to make her feel worse. I told her with care and gentleness, "It's all right, Mama. We forget sometimes." She smiled and thanked me.

Shane had to go to school, and I had to go to work the next morning. I made sure she had everything she needed from me, and then drove back home. I was tired—but satisfying Mama meant more to me than my feelings, my inconvenience. I knew she was aging, and there was no turning back. I never liked leaving her alone; I never felt comfortable about that.

Mama and I talked a lot on the phone. Our conversations covered so many things about life and whatever was going on. Even after I moved back closer to her after all the years of living far away, we still talked on the phone for hours at a time. Sometimes, Mama or I would fall asleep. After waking up and realizing that the other one had fallen asleep too, the phone still in her hand, I would say, "Mama," calling her instead of hanging up the phone because she had gone off to dreamland. At the time, I felt I was keeping her company and engaged. I felt better talking with her on the phone if I could not be at her house — she lived in a rural area in the same house where I grew up. She had no fear about living alone, but with the sentimental heart that I had no power over, I thought of her living alone often. I knew she loved her privacy.

Now I can honestly say, she kept *me* company. I absorbed so much knowledge, and although it was not her intention, she helped me know whom I could trust (or could not trust) based on the characteristics she observed in people. Mama would tell me stories from years ago as well as current events. I remember her telling me about the games she attended as a young woman and the fun she had. We'd talk on the phone for hours about so many things and people in general. It was interesting to hear that because while living at home, we watched so many games on television — basketball, football, and baseball. We were sports fans because of her. If I were to bet on a sport, I'd bet that basketball was Mama's favorite. She'd get caught up in the action and yell, "Make that basket!" or "He fouled!" or "Those boys are playing that ball!"

Out of twelve children, only a few of us played on a school team, not that the talent wasn't there. David was quite athletic, good at football and baseball, and played in a league during his years in school. Charlotte was athletic too, and her sports of choice were volleyball and basketball. I liked softball but never played on a team. Although only a few of us played on a sports team, we kept up with various sports events.

Mama Never Liked Being "Managed"

Mama sometimes stared at me. I suppose she was reflecting, and I usually displayed a calm, amicable spirit, trying to please her and keep the atmosphere pleasant and even humorous many times. I would like to believe that I reminded Mama of herself . . . some aspects of her characteristics. She had told me a few times over the years that I was "different," that I was not as controlling as a few of her other children. I never understood how children think that they can boss their parents around and try to control what they do and say with no regard for their feelings. Aging parents will eventually need their children's guidance and assistance, but there should be a gentleness while doing it. Mama had been a strong, independent woman for so long, and it was a very bad pill for her to swallow when she had to do what someone else told her to do, especially her children. Some of my siblings spoke to Mama harshly and abruptly. If I were around to witness, I defended her, or they would simply not raise their voices at all because they knew I would speak up against it. A few were strong-willed for whatever reasons, perhaps a part of their character. Some exuded patience and some did not. I've always had enormous patience relative to Mama. I believed my siblings loved her as I did but just had adversarial ways of showing it and selfishly wanted things their way instead of honoring her wishes and what she had expressed to us all the years of our lives. I discovered that children can be raised by the same parent(s), but each one will travel their own road, their own direction, despite what they were taught. I despised their behavior toward Mama as she needed personal care. Parents are to be respected, no matter what their circumstances are.

"Honor thy father and thy mother; that thy days may be long upon the land which the Lord thy God giveth thee." —*Exodus 20:12*

I recall when Mama didn't want to take a trip to the Caribbean Island with one of my siblings and a few other people after Jacob married. She had been a few times before with the same group of people (a few of her children and one or more of my brother's friends) for vacation, but after a while, she didn't feel like traveling and preferred to be at home. I understood completely, but a few siblings insisted that she go; they made her go. I often think about older people's mental and physical condition when they are uncomfortable or unhappy about something. Could their heart be stressed? Could they be depressed from realizing that they no longer have control of their life? Life is no longer as they knew it. I couldn't be with Mama all the time. I still had Shane to care for, plus I worked, but when I was in her presence, I defended her honor and protected her from siblings' *foolishness*.

There is a respectable, right way to treat parents or aging or sick adults. They don't operate with the same alertness and mental capacity as when they were young, and require much patience and loving care. They are still human. God gifts each of us with different things, and one of my God-given gifts is to care about others' feelings and to serve others. I wish I'd had the time and resources to take care of Mama. Some people set up roadblocks for selfish gain. I didn't know how devilish and selfish some people could be, but I would soon find out.

Relocating to the same city where Paige was attending college had huge advantages. Shane and I visited Paige often on campus. We'd eat in the campus cafeteria with her, and sometimes wait until she got out of class to spend some time with her. She always kept us in the loop about events on campus and in the city. We met her friends and had really fun times. She stayed connected and included her brother in everything possible. Paige quickly got involved with her school's football program, working in the head coach's office. She got to know the football players, and she made long-lasting friendships with many of them. Shane was interested in playing football so there were so many advantages to his sister working with the football team. It was good for Shane. Paige took him to games and all types of college events. She really looked out for her brother. All the while, their sibling relationship became stronger and stronger.

We'd visit Mama often. We had lived in faraway states like Wyoming and Louisiana, and it was such a welcome change to be able to drive only thirty minutes or less to see Mama. No more once- or twice-per-year trips to see her because we lived so many hours away. All those years I called her almost daily. I would have done anything within my power for her.

FINISHING WHAT I STARTED

When I learned that the healthcare company I was working for had an educational program that allowed employees to take college classes which the company would pay for, I jumped right on it. During orientation for my new position, the trainer told me about the advantages and the rules surrounding it. What a blessing! I looked at the opportunity as a win-win and signed up immediately. I would have been a fool not to take advantage of the opportunity, and Mama didn't raise a fool.

Now I had a daughter in college and a son at home. I suddenly experienced what Mama went through when I was younger and living at home—raising a child, taking college classes full time, working full time, and supporting my college student-daughter in every way I could. Let's not forget that I had only two children, while Mama had five or six at home while she worked full time and was simultaneously enrolled in college. Her challenges were far greater than mine. Dedication and commitment to family and the future were important. I knew that Mama would approve with glee that I was returning to college to complete my degree. Her desire was for all her children to attain at least an undergraduate degree . . . no matter their major of choice. Whenever I would talk with her about working, going to class, supporting my children, and the challenges with juggling it all, she would say over and over again, "If I did it, you can too. Never stop until you finish what you started."

Strength, stamina, perseverance, determination, commitment, destination drive, love for education, excelling, and mountaintop faith were in Mama's spirit like I'd never seen. I didn't need a hero figure. I didn't need a mentor. I just looked to Mama. I had Mama on my mind most of the time while completing my undergraduate degree. I had disappointed her all those many years ago. I needed that degree for more reasons than one, and I needed to complete my degree while Mama was still living and would know that I had. As I was studying and focusing to complete my degree, which meant taking a full course load while working full time, family betrayal was hard at work . . . as hard as I was studying to finish school.

Am I My Brother's Keeper?

I have learned many things about loyalty, who's worthy of your trust, who's dependable, etc. You even learn who will be there for you through thick and thin. It's not automatic for siblings and even parents in some situations to be loyal. It shouldn't even be a question, but that is simply not reality. The family dynamics are simply that, dynamic.

I've had the experience of a "consistently supportive" sibling, Marshall. We've supported one another for a very long time, which doesn't mean there have not been flawed behavior and fall-outs between us. She did things that I adamantly disagreed with and vice versa, but we always managed to come back to the table and move on cordially, as genuine friends do. Life would have been extremely hard without her. I know God impacted our sisterhood and strengthened it to what it is today. Mama knew about how close we were. She knew we had a bond. Marshall and I tried to have the same type of relationship with our other siblings, but the personalities varied greatly. There was no loyalty, and "consistent, reliable support" was a rarity.

Some people envy large families. They should not. The size of the family is irrelevant; the love and support factors are key. I was betrayed so many times. I have been lied to and put in predicaments more than once, and I didn't know about it until months later. Regrettably, Mama didn't consistently teach us throughout childhood to love and support one another no matter what. But she didn't teach us *not* to love one another either. It was perhaps an area of life she didn't focus on at the time. After all, she had so much on her plate for so very long. She had so many things occupying her mind . . . twelve children, twelve lives. Our family structure and experiences are not extraordinary, actually. I believe, based on friends' stories, that "Life" happens in all families. Mama didn't have a warm and fuzzy family life with her own parents and siblings.

However, Marshall and I vowed to break that curse while raising our children. We had dealt with family members who discounted us and talked about us behind our backs rather than give us a call and support us at times when we desperately needed them. I don't even recall hearing "I'll pray for you" or "Let's get together and talk" during my life challenges. I was/am totally opposite of that when it comes to supporting family and encouraging them. If I am not able to see you in person, I'll call or send a message of encouragement.

Paige and Shane have been raised to be quite the opposite. They are very close and rely on one another for support and assistance with whatever comes up in their lives. I told them early on to never abandon the other; to have an honest, dependable relationship; and to never allow anyone to come between them. Paige is older than Shane. While a very young girl and the only child, she asked her dad and I for a brother or a pet. The pet option did not win during that period of our lives. Neither her dad nor I responded favorably to the idea of expanding our family, but we realized that she needed a sibling. Her dad and I wanted a son as well, so it was time to work on it.

Paige was visiting her grandparents out of town for a few weeks during the summer. I called her at her their house and told her the exciting news. She responded just as we thought she would. I felt her joy through the phone. She couldn't wait to be a big sister. I told her that I couldn't guarantee that I'd have a boy, yet in my heart of hearts, I knew I had a boy on the way. Her dad doubted my assurance until I received the sonogram results. That was an exciting time in our lives.

Paige named her brother with our approval. She was a part of doing just about everything for him. I could see early on that helping us with Shane in every aspect of life was important to her. She was his protector, his teacher, and she loved him dearly . . . still does. Paige has included Shane in her life (attending ball games, introducing him to her friends, going to the state fair, sitting together in church) in ways that many sisters would not take the time to do. And when her dad and I divorced, their dependence on one another became even greater. Their dad and I encouraged it. We provided the circumstances for them to remain close right into adulthood, and as adults they are still a phenomenal brother/sister duo. They truly are exemplary for being a "Brother's/Sister's Keeper." They have always known that I have their backs; no one comes before my children when they need me. They know they are loved, and that I would interrupt or even put my life agenda on ice to be wherever they need me to be. I want them to know that I'm available. Now that life has happened to both me and Marshall in ways that would take the rest of our lives to tell, I am in touch with the fact that God knew Marshall and I would need each other, and so did Mama. I have several sisters and brothers. There were times when I felt like I had none. But I never stopped loving them. And I always prayed for them.

My Divine Assignment

Many years ago, I began sending inspirational and encouraging daily messages to family and friends via email, and eventually converted to texting my messages. I sent messages about all sorts of things, but the main objective was to encourage the recipients to be strong, pursue their dreams, love unconditionally, remain faithful no matter their adversity, and keep God in every aspect of their lives.

Several of my siblings complained about my regular messaging. Texting was not so popular initially, and it took some getting used to for many. I loved the new technology because I was able to do something "positive" in bulk. Compared to emails, text messages were right up my alley . . . so much more convenient and less formal. Mama never had the opportunity to use a cell phone, but if she had, I probably would have been scolded for the number of times per day that I sent messages to her. I love writing my thoughts and sharing them, but my sole objective is to encourage and inspire others.

So many of my family and friends are encouraged by my messages. I am very often told, "Don't stop sending them," "You made my day," or, "I needed to hear that today." That inspires me to continue to be a vessel of hope and source of information about God's love for them, and to trust Him and not ever lose faith. My messages are not only about God and praying. I also send messages about what's going on in the world of business, politics, and life in general. I enjoy doing it. I never allow negativity to discourage me and want to spread my positive energy among others. I knew early on that it was my Divine appointment to send God's word to others as well as information that benefitted them.

As years passed, almost all the recipients started to look forward to my messages and commented that they made a difference in their day. It wasn't long before cell phone companies became competitive and phone plans emerged that included unlimited texting and unlimited data usage. That was right up my alley. As I continue doing what I know God assigned me to do, many cannot fathom how I could continue being dedicated to doing it for so long. I knew it was my assignment; that is the only way I can explain it. It has never felt like a burden; it comes easily for me, and I have not stopped in almost twenty years. Over the years, people have been in awe of my persistence and consistency with sending messages to them. I recall when a few siblings and friends told me, "You've been doing that for a very long time." I told them that it doesn't seem that it has been that long. I confidently told them that it must be my Divine appointment. I recall reading about Divine appointments after a few years of beginning my journey to send messages; I learned in my church that when God wants us to do something, He has a way of making sure we do it. He knows who will be obedient and who will do the service well in His name.

God knows what He is doing when He assigns a job to one of His children. How can anyone know or be sure of their divine appointment? Well, if you have an intimate relationship with God, you recognize the gentle whisper of His voice. He speaks to your heart. You are given the "tools" to do it. God does not tell you to do something without equipping you with everything you need to do it. He even places the right people to support you. Everything seems to feel right. The appointment feels so natural while doing it that it comes easily to your spirit.

God only assigns a task to the Christian whom He knows will do it diligently and without feeling burdened. I have never felt burdened or confused about doing the work of the Lord. It helps that I am a writer/journalist at heart and have the skillset to write; I feel every word in every message and ask God to guide me along the way. Nothing was texted to anyone without proper research and confirming the information. No one has ever debated me about the content of my messages, and I have quite a few devoted Christian readers who not only go to church regularly but also read the Bible regularly. I constantly get responses such as, "Amen," "Grateful," "Glory to God," etc. Christians don't normally argue with Scripture. Sometimes, I simply text, "Be safe," "Don't forget to pray," "Eat healthily and stay hydrated," or "Pray for guidance and wisdom." I want to share a positive message or share a teachable moment and more than anything; my objective is to impart words that would inspire their readers to trust God whom we serve and to never lose faith. I know that I have touched lives over the years; I've also benefitted by encouraging myself with my own messages.

"As I minister to you, I minister to myself." —*Lyrics from gospel song, "Encourage Yourself"*

Here are a few of the messages that I have sent over time to my family:

1. There is nothing in your life—no circumstance, no question—that God cannot answer. Ask Him; believe what He says. The Holy Spirit will show you every single thing to do in every situation. Man is okay to confer with, but always ask God first. Your friends and family can support you and advise you, but only God controls the beginning, middle, and the end of all things, no matter what it is. Trust Him as your Counselor. Bless your journey.

2. No matter how popular and powerful some people think they are, there's a Higher Power that supersedes their "vain thoughts and actions." In time, He will reveal himself to them in a pronounced way to teach them a valuable lesson. Observe, learn, and remain humble yourself. Never doubt His power.

3. The most powerful thing in the human psyche is what you think of yourself . . . no matter how others think of you and treat you. What are you allowing? Who are you in Christ? That's what matters. Define your purpose with God's guidance.

4. Nugget of Wisdom: Share your Biblical wisdom about forgiveness with others. Tell them that unforgiveness is toxic and cancerous to the soul. Tell them that without

forgiveness, there is no future for them because with God, it's that serious—unforgiveness is an opening for Satan to derail us from a relationship with God. God is the one to hold people accountable, not us. Help others to understand that it's sinful to hold something over anyone's head or to live begrudgingly. Many Scriptures direct Christians to forgive one another. Ephesians 4:32, for example, states, "Be kind and compassionate to one another, forgiving each other, just as in Christ God forgave you." Tell people that unforgiveness separates them from a life of freedom. By the way, tell yourself.

5. *The Lord's loving-kindnesses indeed never cease, for His compassions never fail. They are new every morning; great is Your faithfulness.*

—Lamentations 3:22-23

6. One of my inspirational messages sent to family on January 31, 2017:

Everyone has gone through something that changed them in such a way that disallows them to be the same ever again. If not, keep living. I have no regrets for my experiences because they made me stronger, more faithful. I certainly know whom to trust, and it surely ain't Man. I do "more of His work" in gratitude for bringing me through several things, and I have received "Double for My Trouble." God is better than good; He's magnificent!

7. Inspirational message sent to family on January 29, 2017:

> *I hope that I'm able to send daily messages for decades more. I've been sending them for about fifteen years (started sending via email before texting became popular). But one thing I know for sure: God, if no one else, will always remember my messages. It's one of my legacies, but it's not just about me. You see, since I'm doing it for good and not to harm, for God and not evil, blessings will continually flow. My children, my grandchildren, and others will benefit far beyond my lifetime. It'll be the Lord's Blessing, coupled with their own commitment to God. Honor God "now" in a way that will continue to help others long after you're gone. Be a stakeholder for God and His Kingdom. Always pray for guidance & wisdom.*

I always end my messages with, "Peace," "Bless your journey," "Carpe diem," or simply, "Love, Goya."

I PRAYED FOR MY CHILDREN

I have often been complimented about doing a great job raising my children. I really cannot say enough about my children, and not only by my prideful estimation. Their daily life decisions prove it, and people have complimented both of them, their dad, and me throughout our lives. We raised them with the forethought that we were raising them not for ourselves—but for the world. They would only be with us as children for a short period of time, and then someday they would be grown and take part in a society that would judge them. We wanted them to be the best example and representation of a woman and man. We knew someday they might be someone's wife, husband, coworker, neighbor, and more. I personally knew that I had to get it right, and with God's guidance.

Mama did not raise me solely to prepare me for adulthood. She knew that it was probable that I would have children on my own someday. Mama wanted her children to have children that would not only be proud of us but also be proud of themselves as respectful, productive Christians. She instilled the importance of education, working hard for a better life, saving money for a rainy day, and treating others the way that we want to be treated. I certainly did not miss any opportunity to teach my children all the same. And the best lesson, as I knew from Mama, was to lead my children by example. If I made a mistake along the way, I archived it only for a time; and at appropriate times, as Mama did with me, I instructed my children to do better than I had done. Paige and Shane didn't get into trouble in school before they left home for college. They were very good "students" in school and at home.

Walter spent quality time with our children as they were growing up. I remember his conversations with Paige about the importance of being honest and doing her best in school. He was a scholarly student himself while in secondary school and in college. Walter often helped Paige to do her homework and prepare for tests. We often split homework duty—Walter assisted her with math and science classes, and I with English, spelling, and her other classes. He made sure that there was available money for Paige to participate in extracurricular activities such as the marching band, dance classes, and piano lessons. I registered her for everything her scheduled allowed, and Walter attended to see her progress and her "final bow" for the season.

Then, when Shane was born, there were the four of us. We doted on Shane all the time. Walter and I enjoyed watching our two children grow up together. Walter would take Shane outside while he mowed the lawn, washed the vehicles, and cooked on the grill. Walter bought Shane a toy grill so he could pretend that he was grilling food as his dad was. That was a comical scene. Shane flipped his plastic, burger patties and hot dogs as if they were really cooking. He was mimicking what he saw his dad do . . . in many ways. Walter and Shane watched many sports events together. He taught his son how to skate and so much more. Shane had many of his dad's characteristics that I see even today. Even your worst self can stay focused for two good reasons. My two reasons were Paige and Shane. Remembering all the things Mama taught me helped in a grand way,

My older brothers often told me, "You raised your kids well." My sisters have said, "You did a good job. They are good kids." I know I did a phenomenal job. I see evidence of it daily. A mother knows. How did I do it? I didn't do it alone. I know God showed me what to do. I am grateful He showed all of us favor, grace, and mercy. What some people don't understand is that all our days were not perfect, but my children were and still are my life. What is perfect, anyway?

The one thing I know for sure is that our perspective on life is valuable. When we keep God in everything and look forward to each day, remarkable things happen. Some might say, "I don't know how I got through this or that." Well, it was God who kept you from losing your mind, from giving up. I am a firm believer. Many times I just had to trust God; there was no other way. He has gotten me through many storms in my life. I've failed, but I have also had victories. God was with me through it all, and His timing is perfect. I learned that I could do nothing on my own strength but rather with His. I am so very grateful for what He has done in my children and my life. I prayed to God many years ago, "Lord, if I don't get anything else right, please make sure I do a great job raising my children." He answered my prayer.

"Have I not commanded you? Be strong and courageous! Do not tremble or be dismayed, for the Lord your God is with you wherever you go." —Joshua 1:9

"Train up a child in the way he should go, and when he is old he will not depart from it." —Proverbs 22:6

"For this child I prayed, and the LORD hath given me my petition which I asked of him." —1 Samuel 1:27-28

MAMA WAS IMPORTANT TO ME

Mama was progressing into memory loss, but I didn't recognize it too much in the beginning. I was not around her on a daily basis. She was still functioning well and caring for herself, driving, shopping, etc. She was substitute teaching at local schools. Some of us children would visit regularly. Since I lived closer to her, I visited often. I called almost daily and sometimes more than once per day. I thought that I was being the daughter that I was supposed to be; I thought I was loving my mama as a daughter should. I have a heart that opens up easily to love and care about others, especially Mama. But negativity was high and wide in my family, pathetically so. Anything that I intended for good was twisted and mangled to something that was not of me; it has never been my intention to harm anyone. I'm just not "cut" like that. I've never been a selfish person or someone who had an ulterior motive. I suppose if others thought that way, their attempt was to impose their way of thinking on others for some agenda or another.

Everyone is unique; no one is a clone of another, but dear God, I'm so grateful I do not share the characteristics of some other people. Mama knew each of her children. Parents who spend significant time with their children know who they are. Very early on, she was able to identify the thing that would either propel us to success or cause ourselves (and her) headaches. Mothers are very good at projecting while praying for the best outcomes. Mama could look at a girl and tell if she was sexually active. She would say, "Once a girl gets with a boy, you can't tell her anything." She meant that the girl's head becomes so wrapped around the boy and the sexual experience, she believes that she's in love and becomes blind to reality and her purpose. It was easy for Mama to figure out what her daughters were up to or had done. Yes, Mama could *read* each of her children very well. I hated it when she looked at me with disappointment. It mattered to me how my mistakes made her feel.

SECRETS KEPT ABOUT MAMA'S HEALTH

At some point, while my daughter Paige was in college and my son Shane was approaching middle-school years, Charlotte was visiting Mama on what seemed to be a weekly or biweekly basis. Neither she nor any sibling who lived out of town had done this before, causing me and other siblings to be concerned. After all, if Mama needed special attention or help with anything, a few of her children, including me, lived closer to her than Charlotte. It was more sensible for us to know what was going on.

At times, no one even knew Charlotte was at Mama's house. On an occasion or two, I went to visit Mama and found out that Charlotte was there. It became a phenomenon to a few of us that her visits were a secret. Why wasn't Charlotte telling us that she was home? Was something medically wrong with Mama? And if Mama was ailing with something, she needed care around the clock, not just when Charlotte was in town. Logic just was not playing a role—kept secrets were not unusual in our family, but I was not happy with Charlotte's secretive behavior. Mama was the mother of all twelve of us, and it was unfair to keep us in the dark. But things began to unfold as everything does, even when done in an atmosphere of darkness. I was the only daughter who lived nearby, only half an hour away from Mama's house at the time; a few brothers lived nearby as well. One brother lived in the same town as Mama, and even he was puzzled. It made sense to keep us in the loop so we could help Mama while Charlotte was not there. Charlotte lived in another state seven to eight hours away.

I called Mama on a few occasions to let her know I was coming to visit her. I never just dropped in on Mama; we were taught to respect her privacy and to check if she was home or felt like seeing anyone before coming to visit. It was one of Mama's lessons in her proper etiquette book. On one occasion while visiting with Mama, Charlotte drove in the yard. I was surprised because I didn't know she was in town. I was glad to see her of course, but I was puzzled about the "secret visit."

Charlotte was cordial as usual, but there was obviously reason for me to show concern because she didn't tell me she was at Mama's house. I had no idea at the time that she was home for reasons that every one of Mama's children should have known about. Mama had an uncomfortable expression on her face and didn't look pleased about the situation, whatever was going on.

I noticed yellow sticky notes on the television in the living room and in other rooms in the house. It was strange. Why were there notes with instructions about TV channels, turning off the stove, locking the door, etc.? I asked Charlotte what was going on, but she dismissed my concern. *But whenever 2+2 doesn't equal 4, there is a reason.* And the reason is the missing part of the equation that someone does not want you to know. Charlotte loved and cared for Mama very well while visiting her. None of us siblings disputed that. But I just could not understand the reason for the secrecy.

After Benjamin, one of our older brothers, heard that Charlotte was back in town again so soon, he came to Mama's house to visit while Charlotte and I were there. He, like myself, didn't understand what was going on. Benjamin took Charlotte to another room to ask her privately if anything was going on that he needed to know. He knew that Charlotte's frequent secret visits were a red flag and signaled some type of problem, particularly since the children who lived nearby didn't know Charlotte was staying with Mama for days at a time. I don't think Benjamin was satisfied with Charlotte's answers, but he stayed only a short while.

It remained a mystery, but not for long. Unfortunately, Mama was caught in the middle of her own children's madness that would divide the family in an unforgettable way—a way that did not have to happen had selfishness, deceitfulness, greed, and betrayal not played roles in some of my siblings' decisions.

THE CAT IS OUT OF THE BAG

Life kept passing us by. In a large family, so much can go on from one year to the next. Mama was showing signs of decline more and more. The secrets kept brewing in a family pot of turmoil and confusion. Communication was lousy, and trust was slim pickings. Selfishness and deceit were so thick anyone could cut them with a knife. Mama was acting less and less like herself. But I didn't know the underlying reasons other than she was aging and slowing down.

Mama was still living alone. Jacob was in town, and I drove to Mama's to see him. After getting there, I learned he had already left to visit our brother, Benjamin. Jacob later called and asked me to pack clothes for Mama because he was taking her on vacation. He had vacationed to the same place yearly a few times before; Mama had been with him, along with his wife, other siblings, and friends.

After having a meal with Mama and relaxing, she and I went to her bedroom to begin packing. Mama was sort of quiet, but in a pleasant mood. She lay on her bed while I made clothing selections for her. I would check with her about what she wanted me to pack. I wanted to respect her wishes and get her approval. In the middle of taking things from her drawer, I asked her if she was okay. She smiled and said, "Yes." I didn't say it to her, but I wanted to travel with her. I always had a protective feeling for her, but never told her. She appeared pleased with me being with her. I was happy to help her prepare for the trip.

As I glanced back at her while I gathered items from her dresser drawer, she appeared to have a glossy, distant look in her eyes. With a smile, she asked me, "What's your name?"

I actually started laughing because I figured she was playing a joke. I responded, "Mama, you know who I am. Stop playing." A look of confusion came over her; she said that she didn't know me, that I looked like her sister Eva's daughter. This took me aback. Still not knowing what was happening, I said, "Mama, I'm your daughter."

What I next heard out of Mama's mouth threw me for a loop, and it's a conversation that I'll never forget. Mama said, "You're not my daughter. You look like my daughter, but you're not." She spoke her words not with nastiness but with confusion. I again told her I was her daughter. My heart was broken because she was so serious about not knowing me. Her memory of me was gone. My heart started beating faster, and my mind started doing many unfamiliar things because I felt lost about what to do. Not knowing the depth of her confusion nor if it was the onset of something medical, I did not go on trying to prove who I was. But Mama followed up with, "I'm going to tell my children what a nice lady you have been to me."

I'll never, ever forget her words. It was a pivotal moment for me. I felt emotions that life had not prepared me for. My mama was not the same as before. What was I to do? I felt lost and helpless.

Strangely, I began hurting for her, not for myself. My mama was lost; her mind was no longer functioning normally. I knew I had to do something quickly. I concluded that she should not be going out of town on a vacation, not even riding with Jacob back to his house. She needed to see her doctor. My mama was suffering an illness that I had to accept. I really became nervous. I told Mama that I was going in the kitchen to get something, but what I really did was call Marshall to tell her what had just happened. I needed help. I needed support and guidance.

I was alone with Mama, and I had no one in the house

to help me cope. I cannot recall what we specifically talk-ed about, but I'm sure Marshall could detect my nervous-ness and some degree of devastation. After all, Mama just told me that I was not her daughter, which hit me hard in the gut. But I did what I knew to do: I said, "Help me, Jesus."

Then, I called Jacob and told him what happened, and that it was not a good idea to take her traveling until we figure out what was going on with her. He became agitat-ed. *Red Flag #2:* He asked me if I had told anyone else. I got the sense that he was hiding something, that he didn't like it that I had told anyone about what had happened with Mama. I told him that I told Marshall. With more frustration, he told me that he would be at Mama's the next morning; he spent the night at Benjamin's house.

I spent the night with Mama, sleeping in the bed with her, but I could not rest. I cried silently. I prayed for Mama and wondered why Jacob was agitated rather than supportive about my experience or showing concern for *our mama.* I had trusted that he would be a voice of reason based on past conversations we had had through-out our lives.

Mama and I continued talking about different things. Somehow, I knew not to upset her by continually telling her that I was her daughter. Mama was in her late seven-ties at that time. She needed no stress. I continued caring for her and talking with her until she fell asleep. I was in-creasingly becoming perplexed and protective of Mama, anxious to get help for her.

I wish I knew then what I know now about why she could not rest. The illness had caused an avalanche of problems for her brain function. I reflected on Grandma and how Mama was concerned about her so many years before when Grandma was suffering from memory loss. I was not even a teenager then. Mama wanted her to live with us, but Grandma, as with many aging adults, did not want to leave her home. During my reflection on all the things that happened during those years, I wondered if the same could be happening to Mama. Years ago, memory loss in an elderly person was called "senility," which Merriam-Webster defines as *the quality or state of being senile: the physical and mental decline associated with old age; especially the deterioration of cognitive functioning associated with old age.*

Morning came. Something told me to write down all the company names, addresses, and phone numbers from Mama's mail that I saw in her bedroom. I even wrote down the balances and face values of her insurance policies and the beneficiaries. Mama had investment accounts with significant balances. My instinct kicked in to take notes of everything that I saw—if Mama would no longer be the strong, independent woman I had known, I had to be proactive with her personal business affairs. I knew that phone calls would have to be made as well as business decisions if she no longer could conduct business based on her prognosis. I didn't tell Jacob or anyone that I had the information. I put the information in a safe place, not knowing that it would become so handy in the future. And wow . . . did it ever.

Jacob arrived at Mama's, and oh boy, our relationship changed that day. We didn't agree about several things concerning Mama. I admit that both Jacob and I were very strong-willed and relentless about what to do with her. I recall all the unpleasantries. When he wanted things done his way, there was discord when anyone disagreed with him. I can recall thinking that perhaps if Dad were still living and had been a different type of husband and father, the predicaments that would follow would not have even been a concern. So many times, as an adult, I wished that some of my siblings were more supportive of us as a whole family . . . the right way, a way that would have disallowed adverse behavior and absence from the *wrong* that was taking place right before their eyes. All I ever wanted for Mama was for her to be safe, healthy, and happy. I believed that it was our responsibility as her children to make decisions that aligned with her welfare as she continued to age and decline. And it needed to be done together as a family, not just by a few of her children.

Mama had taught us to do what's right so there wouldn't be any regrets later. Despite her teachings, all of us have fallen short. I know that God gave me a different kind of heart. I have done things the wrong way in my lifetime just as anyone else. I've had to ask God for forgiveness, and I've had to forgive those who have wronged me. But I can confidently say that I have never taken anything from my mama or intentionally done anything to undermine her, my siblings, or anyone else. Mama struggled for years to accumulate the things she had, and she saved her money. Mama was a hard worker and a planner. She did not squander money to impress others, but she lived well as life moved along for her, and she only wanted a good life for her children, something that Dad cared less about. The devil had such a strong hold on a few family siblings . . . perhaps more than a few. As a strong Christian today, I know that Mama prayed for all of us while she also cried for all of us. I cried during those times . . . so many times . . . for Mama and for my family. So much happened that should not have.

"Stop your crying and wipe away your tears. All that you have done for your children will not go unrewarded. They will return from the enemy's land. There is hope for your future. Your children will come back home. I, the Lord, have spoken." —Jeremiah 31:16-17

"Children, obey your parents in the Lord, because this is right. Honor your father and mother which is the first commandment with a promise—that it may go well with you and that you may have a long life." —Ephesians 6:1-3

"Honor your father and mother. Then you will live a long, full life in the land the LORD your God will give you." —Exodus 20:12

Jacob's behavior was sometimes unpredictable. At times he could be so kind, helpful, and easy to get along with, as well as be a great listener and advisor for the family. His support was more than admirable during periods of my life and others in our family. He was intelligent and had a fierce drive to succeed by any means. His knowledge did not stem from a wealth of degrees or skill sets; he was an avid reader and kept the company of well-educated people and people who held high positions in their respective careers, giving him access to many opportunities. He sought knowledge by way of "untraditional" means. Mama would describe that as "rubbing elbows" with certain types of folks. Jacob had been, from a boy, a person who wanted to excel. He was never a follower. Jacob not only dreamed of things he wanted to accomplish, he executed his plans; he never gave up, and I know very well where his drive came from — our mama. I was proud of Jacob for years, and we had talked about so much as children. We wanted to go far in life. And we have . . . and we are still moving.

Unfortunately, when the other side of Jacob showed up, it was like anger rising from the darkest pit. Make no mistake, my brother is a Christian; he believes in a higher power. When we do things less than respecting of what God teaches us in the Bible, we have lost our way, but God can help us get back on track *if* we seek His guidance and wisdom. It's never, ever too late. That's what having faith is all about.

"Let us examine and probe our ways, and let us return to the Lord." —Lamentations 3:40

"For which of you, desiring to build a tower, does not first sit down and count the cost, whether he has enough to complete it?" —Luke 14:28

"And he made from one man every nation of mankind to live on all the face of the earth, having determined allotted periods and the boundaries of their dwelling place, that they should seek God, and perhaps feel their way toward him and find him. Yet he is actually not far from each one of us." —Acts 17:26-27

"The steps of a man are established by the Lord, when he delights in his way; though he fall, he shall not be cast headlong, for the Lord upholds his hand." —Psalm 37:23-24

———————————

As Jacob came inside Mama's house that day, his expression of calm gave no indication of what was to come. He chatted for a few minutes with Mama and me before asking me to go outside with him. At that point, I figured that he wanted to further discuss what I experienced with Mama the night before and what we needed to do about it next. As we were walking to the door, Mama asked, "Are y'all leaving?" I told her that I was going back home, and Jacob told Mama that he'd be back. I assumed that he would do the right thing and take her to her doctor or have her assessed by a professional before taking her out of town.

Red Flag #3: Once outside, Jacob said, "I didn't like it

when you told me last night that Mama shouldn't go on the trip with me."

I was perplexed, and surely it showed. My recommendation for Mama not to travel before knowing what was going on with her health was more important to me than his ego. "Obviously, she is not functioning in normal capacity as we know her to do," I said.

Jacob and I started arguing and he audaciously said, "Get out of my yard." Well, I was at Mama's house, in her yard. I thought what he said was not only bold but ludicrous. I'm sure I responded with choice, "un-Christian-like" words the more my anger grew and the more stupidly he spoke to me. I'd told Mama I was going back home after I talked with Jacob, and so I'd already said goodbye to her. Throughout the fiasco, I kept looking back at the door, wondering if Mama could overhear us and would come to see what was going on. I'm sure our voices escalated in an angry tone. The conversation was so ridiculous to me! But *why* was Jacob reacting this way?

Mama did open the door, wearing a look of concern. Jacob and I were only a few feet away from the door. Jacob told her that he would be there in a minute. I was infuriated and knew that Mama was in the care of someone making irrational decisions. I was so concerned for her and silently prayed for her health. Needing to get back home and wanting to end the madness with my brother, I got in my truck and cranked it up; he just had to spew one more vile comment, shouting, "And don't come back."

Those words angered me, as he knew that they would. I didn't even place my foot on the brakes before throwing the truck gear in park, which caused the truck to jerk. I opened my truck door with the intent to go back and give Jacob a piece of my mind. He went back into the house, knowing he needed to put much space between us; that was the last straw.

I didn't go after him. He closed the door, which I'm sure he locked behind him in another attempt to humiliate me. Thank the Lord for telling me through the Holy Spirit, "Enough!" I felt I needed to leave and I went home. And the next day, Jacob took Mama on an eight-hour drive to his home. I worried about her for several reasons, which later proved to be valid. I prayed for Mama. I worried about her health condition and how she was going to be treated.

I stayed in constant prayer for Mama. I knew she would be confused about leaving her home. If she didn't recognize me as her daughter, then it was probable she didn't recognize Jacob as her son. Those hours were heart-wrenching for me while imagining her in the car, feeling confused and perhaps afraid. But apparently, Jacob thought he knew better than I did—that Mama would be fine on the trip.

However, Jacob contacted me later and said that I was right: Mama didn't know *who he was either.* Unfortunately, he was already in another city, far from home. Jacob and others had made plans for Mama's life, plans that did not include all of her children's involvement, nor consideration of what she had talked about with us concerning her care—and how she wanted to live her life as she aged.

And so the biggest rift arose among us, and our family life of turmoil began . . . a life that I wish for no one, especially an aging parent. Our mama's life turned into something similar to what she had risen from . . . so I thought.

"Wait on the LORD: be of good courage, and he shall strengthen thine heart: wait, I say, on the LORD."
—Psalm 27:14

"But those who trust in the Lord for help will find their strength renewed. They will rise on wings like eagles; they will run and not get weary; they will walk and not grow weak." —Isaiah 40:31

"Let your hope keep you joyful, be patient in your troubles, and pray at all times." —Romans 12:12

Marshall: Sadly, I rarely see Sophia, the youngest and one I cared for when I was a child. As to the others, for the past ten years, I've only seen them in court and at the funerals of our mother and brother. Everyone but the oldest, Emma, lives less than thirty minutes from me.

MAMA'S TEARS FELT

I thank the Lord for Mama's children's commitment to follow Him despite the many unpleasant events over the years, and for all the times He listens to us when we call His name. We have had a challenging life as a family, and we're no different than the next family. The more we follow Him, the more we'll hear Him speaking to our heart and we'll be guided throughout our life. If we cannot hear the Lord's voice and identify the direction that He wants us to go, perhaps we are not as close to Him as we could be and as He desires. We all should be assured that we're standing on the edge of the greatest chapter in our life; we've not begun to scratch the surface of what we can accomplish for ourselves, how we can support and love our children more than ever, and what we can do for others whom we know and love and those who cross our path.

We cried for Mama for so many reasons: a complex childhood, sisters who didn't

support her, a volatile marriage, children who had her heart aching at times, and discrimination and unfairness on various jobs. And if that wasn't enough — after all that negativity, her children had become grown-ups, but some of them continued to disrespect her and treated her unkindly. Some of them defied everything she had taught them. When parents become senior citizens and can no longer care for themselves, their children should carry out their wishes that they had imparted to them early on. They should even respect the parents' instructions respective to funeral and burial services.

Mama was disrespected *again.* She had already lived with an abusive husband and her older children endured the unthinkable for years. Mama had some good times after Dad died. She was a Christian and introduced her children to God very early in life. We're grateful that Mama knew God and trusted Him. It comforts me that she had the best friend anyone could ever have throughout the years. She gave credence to Him for all that she plowed through in the past.

I'm glad I used rational thinking, made calls, and researched what could be going on with Mama's business affairs. I knew that I would have to get the ball rolling for the woman who not only had the strength and faith to return to college to complete her BS degree after a tumultuous marriage—but also had raised twelve children. Mama had worked various professional jobs and encouraged her children to pursue an education, and she saved quite a bit of money—in fact, thousands of dollars. *Imagine that, after all she had been through.* Mama was smart, and more than that, she was wise.

I told no one that I had saved the information from Mama's mail, but I knew it would come in handy someday. However, what I didn't know was that it would come in handy *legally* to speak the truth about Mama's assets and to vindicate the innocent ones. So much was learned, and several of Mama's children were perceived differently as time went on. Knowledge truly is powerful. Our lives took a different direction. But make no underestimation that I was raised by a very strong woman, and therefore I am strong. *Doubt me at your own peril.*

Joya and *Marshall*

THANKFUL FOR OUR FAITH

As children, we saw Mama cry. As grown women, we saw her cry and cried with her at times— openly and with sensibility and compassion like never before. We knew why she was crying. Because we had similar experiences after becoming wives and mothers, we understood her life's miles.

Mama prayed often. She cried as much at times. We're not only convinced but are faithful witnesses—knowing that God hears our cries and will rescue us and raise us up. There is no doubt in my mind that that is what helped get Mama through tough days.

We have so much more to tell you about Mama and the splintering of our family, along with our many joys and triumphs. Our riveting and compelling story will continue in part two of the *I Know Why Mama Cried* series.

---

www.ingramcontent.com/pod-product-compliance
Lightning Source LLC
Chambersburg PA
CBHW021227090426
42740CB00006B/420